Print Media and Photojournalism

Charles Nandi

Reference Press

4831/24, Ansari Road,
Darya Ganj,
New Delhi-110 002.
Phone: 51563444, 23260807
Fax: 51563334
E-mail: info@essessreference.com
url: www.essessreference.com

First Published : 2006

Rs. 575/-

ISBN: 81-8405-011-9

Published By:
Reference Press
4831/24, Ansari Road,
Darya Ganj,
New Delhi-110 002.
Phone: 23260807, 51563444
Fax: 51563334
E-mail: info@essessreference.com
url: www.essessreference.com

Printed in India at:
Mehra Offset Press, New Delhi.

Contents

Preface

Journalism is a discipline of collecting, verifying, reporting and analyzing information gathered regarding current events, including trends, issues and people. Those who practice journalism are known as journalists. Information is a term with many meanings depending on context but is, as a rule, closely related to such concepts as meaning, knowledge, instruction, communication, representation and mental stimulus. Journalism is moving online rapidly and just as the site of journalism is changing, so is the nature of more future oriented journalism now increasingly being practiced.

News oriented journalism often is described as the 'first draft of history', even though journalists often write news articles bearing deadline in their mind, news media usually edits and proof reads the results prior to publication and this is called print media. In print media, the role of photography is very vital. Photojournalism is a particular form of journalism i.e.: collecting, editing and presenting of news material for publication or broadcast, that creates images in order to narrate a news story. It is now usually understood to refer only to still images and to refer largely to serious news stories.

Print media, a medium that disseminates printed medium, a means or instrumentality for storing or communicating information, press, the gathering and publishing of news in the form of newspapers or magazines.

Photojournalism as a descriptive term often implies the use of a certain bluntness of style or approach to image making. That's why one would not call a normal wedding photographer a photojournalist even though they cover a timely event and their images may be published in the press.

I shall like to thank all those who helped me in writing of this book, this would not have been possible without the support of my daughter Junie, wife Sucheta, mother Mrs. Putul Nandi and father Mr. S.K. Nandi. I shall be failing in my duty if I don't thank Prof. Dr. Tapati Basu, Head, Department of Journalism, Mass Communication and Media Studies, University of Calcutta.

Charles Nandi

1

Introduction to Journalism

Journalism is a discipline of collecting, verifying, analyzing and presenting information gathered regarding current events, including trends, issues and people. Those who practice journalism are known as journalists. News-oriented journalism often is described as the "first draft of history." Even though journalists often write news articles to a deadline, news media usually edit and proofread the results prior to publication.

Journalism has as its main activity the reporting of events — stating who, what, when, where, why and how, and explaining the significance and effect of events or trends. Journalism exists in a number of media: newspapers, television, radio, magazines and, since the end of 20th century, the Internet. Generally, publishers and consumers of journalism draw a distinction between reporting ("just the facts") and opinions (such as editorials, (the official opinions of the paper) and op-ed columns ("opposite the editorial page" commentary)). However, this distinction sometimes can break down.

Journalists may unintentionally fall prey to propaganda or disinformation. Journalists may give a biased account of facts by reporting selectively, for instance, focusing on anecdote or giving partial explanation of actions. Foreign reporting may become more susceptible to bias, because the writers or editors of a newspaper in a given geographical area may find it more difficult to fact-check reports originating at a distance.

Newspapers and periodicals often will contain features written by journalists, many of whom specialize in this form of "in-depth" journalism. Journalists' interaction with sources sometimes involves confidentiality. Many Western governments guarantee the freedom of the press. By extension, these freedoms sometimes also add legal protection for journalists, allowing them to keep the identity of a source private even when demanded by police or prosecutors.

Blogging

Recently there has been some controversy as to whether blogging constitutes a form of journalism. There have been arguments on both sides of the debate further fueled by a March 2005 court ruling in a case involving Apple Computer and several Apple rumor blogs. In that ruling the judge declared that the blogs were not entitled to journalist protections with regards to preserving the anonymity of sources because they don't qualify as a form of journalism. This set a legal precedent that many hope will be reversed on appeal.

Types of Journalism

— Advocacy journalism

— Alternative journalism

— Broadcast journalism

— Business journalism

— Citizen journalism

— Computer-assisted reporting

— Gonzo journalism

— Electronic journalism - news aquisition by means of analogue and digital electronic recording devices.

— Investigative journalism

— Literary journalism related to Creative nonfiction

— Muckraking

— New journalism

— Online journalism

— Photo journalism

— Sports journalism

— Tabloid journalism

— Trade journalism Trade publications covering news specific to industries and professions.

— Yellow journalism

Advocacy Journalism

Advocacy journalism aims to persuade through fact-telling. It rejects the notion of objectivity, instead exposing bias to the reader and expressing explicit opinions on the subject matter. The general goal is to present facts in such a compelling, well-researched manner that even a skeptical reader or one who does not share the writer's opinions, will be swayed to some degree, or at least better informed about the issue at hand.

Advocacy journalism is often practiced in alternative media, including alternative weekly publications. Many of these media outlets have strong political leanings. The genre may extend to a single article in a broader publication; there are also "advocacy journals" or "alternative publications" which announce their intended biases in their mastheads.

One writer for the "alternative" journalism collaborative, the Independent Media Center, writes the following in a call to action: Classic tenets of journalism call for objectivity and neutrality. These are antiquated principles no longer universally observed.... We must absolutely not feel bound by them. If we are ever to create meaningful change, advocacy journalism will be the single most crucial element to enable the necessary organizing. It is therefore very important that we learn how to be successful advocacy journalists. For many, this will require a different way of identifying and pursuing goals.

Objectivity Journalism

Advocacy journalists may reject the principle of objectivity in their work for several different reasons. Many believe that there is no such thing as objective reporting, that there will always be some form of implicit bias, whether political, personal, or metaphysical, and whether intentional or subconscious. This is not necessarily a rejection of the existence of an objective reality, merely a statement about our inability to report on it in a value-free fashion. This may sound like a radical idea, but many mainstream journalists accept the philosophical idea that pure "objectivity" is impossible, but still seek to minimize bias in their work.

Other journalistic standards, such as balance, and neutrality, may be used to describe a more practical kind of "objectivity". "Alternative" critics often charge that the mainstream's media claims of being "bias free" are a harmful because they paper over inevitable (often subconscious) biases, or that they have the effect of advancing certain political ideas which are disguised in an "objective" viewpoint. Critics may contend that the mainstream media reinforce majority-held ideas, marginalizing dissent and harming the larger political and cultural discourse debate and diversity.

The proposed solution is to make biases explicit, with the intention of promoting transparency and self-awareness that better serves media consumers. Advocacy journalists often assume that their audiences will share their biases (especially in politically charged alternative media), or will at least be conscious of them while evaluating what are supposed to be well-researched and persuasive facts. Some who believe that objective (or balanced, neutral, etc.) reporting is possible, or that it is a laudable goal, do not find that striving for objectivity is always appropriate goal, perhaps depending on the publication and the purpose at hand. For example, it might be argued that when attempting to expose a waste, corruption, or abuse, a neutral position would "get in the way" of the exposition, and a "bias" against this kind of criminal activity would be quite acceptable to the intended audience.

Many advocacy journalists claim that they can reject objectivity while holding on to the goals of fairness and accuracy, and claim that corporate journalists often lack both. Computer-assisted reporting is the use of computers to gather news. The spread of computers, software and the Internet is changing how reporters work. Reporters now routinely collect information in databases, analyze public records with spreadsheets and statistical programs, study political and demographic change with geographic information system mapping, conduct interviews by e-mail, and research background for articles on the Web.

Collectively this has become known as computer-assisted reporting, or CAR. It is closely tied to "precision" or "analytic" journalism, which refer specifically to the use of techniques of the social sciences by journalists. CAR's greatest growth has been in recent years, coinciding with the adoption of computers for everyday use. Its roots, however, go back decades. One researcher argues the "age of computer-assisted reporting" began in 1952, when CBS television used a UNIVAC I computer to analyze returns from the U.S. presidential election. One of the earliest examples came in 1967, after riots in Detroit, when Philip Meyer of the Detroit Free Press used a mainframe computer to show that people who had attended college were equally likely to have rioted as were high school dropouts.

The techniques expanded, however, from polling and surveying to a new opportunity for journalists: using the computer to analyze huge volumes of government records. The first example of this type may have been Clarence Jones of The Miami Herald, who in 1969 worked with a computer to find patterns in the criminal justice system. Other notable early practitioners included David Burnham of The New York Times, who in 1972 used a computer to expose discrepancies in crime rates reported by the police; Elliot Jaspin of The Providence Journal, who in 1986 matched databases to expose school bus drivers with bad driving histories and criminal records; and Bill Dedman of The Atlanta Journal-Constitution, who received the Pulitzer Prize for his 1988 investigation of mortgage lending discrimination, or redlining.

In the last 15 years, journalism organizations such as the National Institute for Computer-Assisted Reporting (NICAR, a program of Investigative Reporters and Editors) and the Danish International Center for Analytical Reporting (DICAR), have been created solely to promote the use of CAR in newsgathering. Many other organizations, such as the Society of Professional Journalists and the Canadian Association of Journalists, offer CAR training or workshops.

Investigative Journalism

Investigative journalism and muckraking might be considered forms of advocacy journalism. Investigative reports often focus on illegal or unethical activity, or aim to advance a generally accepted public interest, such as government accountability, alleviation of human suffering, etc. It might be argued that the journalist is assuming a point of view that public action is warranted to change the situation being described.

Many professional journalists and many readers find otherwise standards-adhering and well-researched news and documentary work that dispenses with the notion of journalistic objectivity to be "bad journalism", to be a type of "editorializing" (a serious breach of journalistic protocol), or not to be journalism at all (because it does not follow the standards accepted among mainstream journalists). Some fear that the activity of self-described advocacy journalists to be harmful to the reputation of the mainstream press as an objective, reliable source for information. Another concern is that undiscriminating readers will accept the facts and opinions advanced in advocacy pieces as if they were objective and representative, becoming unknowingly and perhaps dangerously misinformed as a result.

Advocacy journalists vary in their response to these criticisms. Some believe that mainstream and "alternative" outlets serve different purposes, and sometimes different audiences entirely, and that the difference is readily apparent to the public. Many believe that the mainstream press is not an objective and reliable source of information, and so doesn't deserve the reputation it seeks to maintain.

Alternative Media

As long as there has been media there has been alternative media. The line between the two is not always clearly defined. Proponents of alternative media often argue that the mainstream media is heavily biased. Causes of this bias include the political interests of the owners, government influence or the profit motive. While sources of alternative media are also frequently highly (and sometimes proudly) biased, the bias tend to be different, hence 'alternative'.

Authors such as Louis Althusser and Noam Chomsky have written in detail about the problems of the mainstream press, and their writings have inspired the creation of many alternative press efforts. Many current alternative press sources share values on copyright with the open source movement. Examples of alternative media include both print and electronic forms: Z Magazine, Traditions Magazine, Indymedia, CounterPunch, Altermedia and Commondreams. Business journalism includes coverage of companies, the workplace, personal finance, and economics, including unemployment and other economic indicators.

Business coverage gained prominence in the 1990s, with wider investment in the stock market. The Wall Street Journal focuses on business and is one of the USA's top newspapers, in both circulation and respect of journalists. Citizen journalism, also known as "participatory journalism," is the act of citizens "playing an active role in the process of collecting, reporting, analyzing and disseminating news and information," according to the seminal report We Media: How Audiences are Shaping the Future of News and Information, by Shayne Bowman and Chris Willis. They say, "The intent of this participation is to provide independent, reliable, accurate, wide-ranging and relevant information that a democracy requires."

"Public journalism" can refer to this journalism work by ordinary people, or it can mean certain work or aspects of work by professional journalists. The latter meaning is also often called "civic journalism". Citizen journalism usually involves empowering ordinary citizens — including traditionally marginalized members of society — to engage in activities that were previously the domain of professional reporters. "Doing citizen journalism right means crafting a crew of correspondents who are typically excluded from or misrepresented by local television news: low-income women, minorities and youth — the very demographic and lifestyle groups who have little access to the media and that advertisers don't want," says Robert Huesca, an associate professor of communication at Trinity University in San Antonio, Texas.

Citizen journalists may be activists within the communities they write about. This has drawn some criticism from traditional media institutions such as The New York Times, which have accused proponents of public journalism of abandoning the traditional goal of objectivity. Civic journalism refocuses the mission of the news media. According to Edward M. Fouhy of the Pew Center for Civic Journalism, "It is an effort to reconnect with the real concerns that viewers and readers have about the things in their lives they care most about — not in a way that panders to them, but in a way that treats them as citizens with the responsibilities of self-government, rather than as consumers to whom goods and services are sold.

The public journalism movement emerged after the 1988 U.S. presidential election as a countermeasure against eroding trust in the news media and widespread public disillusionment with politics and civic affairs. Jay Rosen, a journalism professor at New York University, was one of its earliest proponents. From 1993 to 1997, he directed the Project on Public Life and the Press, funded by the Knight Foundation and housed at NYU. More recently, he runs the PressThink weblog. Former Wichita Eagle editor Davis "Buzz" Merritt steered his newspaper in a public journalism direction and wrote "Public Journalism and Public Life," published in 1995.

Academics and others who have written about the topic include Ted Glasser, Philip Meyer & his students, Arthur Charity, Lewis Friedland, Jeff Dvorkin, Leonard Witt, Herbert Gans, and Jan Schaffer. Initially, discussions of public journalism focused on promoting journalism that was "for the people" by changing the way professional reporters did their work. In 1998, a study done for the Pew Center and the Associated Press Managing Editors found that "Forty-five percent of all editors surveyed say that their newsrooms use the tools and techniques of civic journalism. Sixty-six percent say they either embrace the label or like the philosophy and tools, suggesting that there are even more practitioners."

According to Leonard Witt, however, early public journalism efforts were "often part of 'special projects' that were expensive, time-consuming and episodic. Too often these projects dealt with an issue and moved on. Journalists were driving the discussion. They would say, 'Let's do a story on welfare-to-work (or the environment, or traffic problems, or the economy)," and then they would recruit a cross-section of citizens and citizens and chronicle their points of view. Since not all reporters and editors bought into public journalism, and some outright opposed it, reaching out to the people from the newsroom was never an easy task." By 2003, in fact, the movement seemed to be petering out, with the Pew Center for Civic Journalism closing its doors.

Simultaneously, however, journalism that was "by the people" began to flourish, enabled in part by emerging internet and networking technologies, such as weblogs, chat rooms, message boards, wikis and mobile computing. In South Korea, Ohmynews became popular and commercially successful with the motto, "Every Citizen is a Reporter." Founded by Oh Yeon-ho on February 22, 2000, it has a staff of some 40-plus traditional reporters and editors who write about 20% of its content, with the rest coming from other freelance contributors who are mostly ordinary citizens. OhmyNews has been credited with transforming South Korea's conservative political environment.

During the 2004 U.S. presidential election, both the Democratic and Republican parties issued press credentials to citizen bloggers covering the convention, marking a new level of influence and credibility for nontraditional journalists. Some bloggers also began watchdogging the work of conventional journalists, monitoring their work for biases and inaccuracy. A recent trend in citizen journalism has been the emergence of what blogger Jeff Jarvis terms hyperlocal journalism, as online news sites invite contributions from local residents of their subscription areas, who often report on topics that conventional newspapers tend to ignore.

Electronic journalism, known as "EJ" or "ENG" for electronic news gathering is most associated with broadcast news where producers, reporters and editors make use of electronic recording devices for gathering and presenting information in telecasts and radio transmissions reaching the public. The acquisition mediums of choice in 2005 are characterized by a variety of competing types or "formats" of video tape Sound recording and editing offer a large number of analogue and digital systems. Still images, graphics and animation have their own sets of tools. The editorial systems available provide journalists with tools for fast and flexible assembly and delivery of electronically gathered and edited news reports.

Video Journalism

News via video is seen daily by millions of people around the world. Some of the typical uses include interviews, panel discussions, press conferences, speeches. Live and pre-recorded video is also used in news coverage of accidents, natural disasters and war coverage. The National Archives of the United States holds a collection of some of earliest examples historically significant motion picture films for the country and similar collections exist in other nation's archives. From the earliest days of the medium's existence, film cameras have been used for the acquisition of news elements and documentary footage.

Film remained important in daily news operations until the late 1960s when news outlets turned to portable video cameras, portable recorders, wireless microphones and joined those with various microwave and satellite linked delivery systems. The 1962 arrival of the "Handy-Looky", a portable video tape camera from Ikegami announced a revolution in journalism. This Handy Looky provided a self-contained system of camera with lens and video recorder, the precursor of today's hand held cameras. As systems have improved, components have been made smaller and lighter and performance has greatly improved. Improvements in image quality, colorimetry, lens types, tape formulation.

- Early formats of video tape — 2 Inch Quad, 1 Inch Video, 3/4 Umatic
- Betacam Tape — Broadcast standard format
- 1080i/720p - High definition video format
- CCD Camera Technology
- DVC Pro format
- Mini DV
- High8
- Editng Systems, Avid, Final Cut Pro, Video Vegas
- Satellite, broadcast, cable, microwave

Photographs, Graphics, Animation

Apart from moving images and sound recording, electronic journalism makes liberal use of still images, graphics and animation in reports.

— In television, still photographs, may be used when no video camera can reach a correspondent or interview subject. A still photograph may also be used to show historically notable person and event or in any place where it aids the report. Photos may be recorded with a standard video camera or the photos can be placed on a special motion control device which allows precise computer controlled positioning. Whether shot in the field or in the studio, the camera operator might zoom, pan or tilt while recording the images. The director may use portions of this video or may digitally store some selected frames for insertion into the final report.

— Graphics are used to report on financial markets, labor statistics, crop reports, municipal budgets and other instances where tabular data or charts are the best choice for explaining a story element. In electronic journalism, graphics are displayed while the reporter continues to read the script. The graphics, including fonts and titles, convey news worthy information, names and titles. The use of graphics also support a station or network's image. Graphics, in some cases, may open up some revenue generating opportunities to the content delivery channel.

— Animation is an effective tool for communicating views of a natural disaster or a tragic accident like a plain crash. Producers might turn to animation to explain a complex scientific process, economic or political polling trends; to illustrate news about space flights and many other appropriate uses.

Meteorologists make use of simple and complex animation to show the path of storms.

Audio Journalism

Radio has long been used to broadcast news as quickly as possible. Many important speeches and public events were covered on radio and still are today. With the growing availability of small, yet high-quality, cassette recorders, such as those from Marantz and Sony, radio reporters are able to make use of natural sounds and interviews which brings great detail to their reports. Creative nonfiction is a genre of literature, also known as literary journalism and narrative journalism, which uses literary skills in the writing of nonfiction. A work of creative nonfiction, if well written, contains accurate and well-researched information and also holds the interest of the reader. Creative nonfiction is contrasted to "research nonfiction" which may contain accurate information, but may not be particularly well written.

Narrative nonfiction is a type of creative nonfiction which tells a story, for example, Black Hawk Down by Mark Bowden. Black Hawk Down began as a series of newspaper and Internet articles. Its availability as an Internet series gave the author the benefit of extensive feedback from viewers. Bob Woodward of the Washington Post is also noted for his skills at narrative nonfiction, in books like All the President's Men and Bush at War.

A wide variety of audio recording formats is use in news rooms around the world. The standard report kit includes a battery operated cassette recorder with a dynamic microphone and optional telephone interface. With this set-up, the reporter can record interviews and natural sound and then play these over a telephone line for rerecording or live broadcast by the content provider (radio or TV station, cable outlet, web radio system). This offers a rugged and relatively simple system which can be placed into a single bag along with extra batteries, tape and supplies.

In addition to the standard compact cassette another popular choice is the digital minidisk. This has the advantage of superior sound, digital indexing and is re-recordable, reusable medium. The small cassette format known as DAT is popular with film makers and other studio professionals because of its superior sound quality and its SMPTE time code and other synchronization features. News gathering may also be accomplished with the use of recordable CD and DVD players and various fixed medium recording system.

New Journalism was the name given to a style of news writing and journalism by Tom Wolfe who, when having trouble writing an assignment, sent his editor an unstructured narrative letter rather than the tight piece usually expected of a journalist of that time. New Journalism took on many of the devices of literary fiction:

— Stream of consciousness

— Conversational speech (rather than quotations and statements)

— Writer's opinions, thoughts and feelings (as opposed only to corroborated facts).

The range of subjects covered by writers writing in the new journalism style covered most areas that journalism would normally cover. The psychedelic movement was something that many of the writers of the period covered, such as in Tom Wolfe's The Electric Kool-Aid Acid Test. The Vietnam War was another common topic. New journalism's techniques were also applied to less obvious subjects, such as financial markets.

Online journalism is reporting and other journalism produced or distributed via the Internet. Many news organizations based in other media also distribute news online. How much they take advantage of the medium varies. Some news organizations use the Web only or primarily. The Internet challenges traditional news organizations in several ways. They may be losing classified ads to Web sites, which are often targeted by interest instead of geography. The advertising on news Web sites is sometimes insufficient to support the investment. Even before the Internet, technology and perhaps other factors were dividing people's attention, leading to more but narrower media outlets.

The Internet has also given rise to more participation by people who aren't normally journalists, such as with Indy Media. Bloggers write on web logs or blogs. Traditional journalists often do not consider bloggers to automatically be journalists. This has more to do with standards and professional practices than the medium. But as of 2005, blogging has generally gained at least more attention and has led to some effects on mainstream journalism, such as exposing problems related to a television piece about President Bush's National Guard Service.

Other significant tool of on-line journalism are Internet forums, discussion boards and chats especially those representing net version of official media. The widespread of Internet all over the World created a unique opportunity to create a meeting place for both sides in many conflicts: Israeli-Palestinian conflict or Russian-Chechen war being worth mentioning. Often this gives a unique chance to find new, alternative solutions to the conflict but often the message boards are turn into the battlefield by contradicting parties creating endless "Online battles"

Most Internet users agree that on-line source is often less biased and more informative then the official media.

This claim is often backed with the belief that on-line journalists are merely a volunteers and free-lancers who are not paid for their activity, and therefore are free from corporate ethics. But recently many internet forums began to moderate their boards because of threat of vandalism, which is seen as an attempt of censorship by many users.

Some Online journalists having an ambition to replace the mainstream media in the long run. Some independent forums and discussion boards have already achieved a level of popularity comparable to the mainstream TV or new agencies. Internet radio, based on the development of home PC based radio station is another growing internet based independent media.

Newsfeeding

The Internet also offers options such as personalized newsfeeds and aggregators such as Google News. As of March 2005, Wikinews rewrites articles from other news organization. Some people see too much personalization as detrimental — for example, that people will have narrower exposure. Photojournalism is a particular form of journalism (i.e., the collecting, editing, and presenting of news material for publication or broadcast) that creates images in order to tell a news story. It is now usually understood to refer only to still images, and to refer largely to serious news stories. Photojournalism is distinguished from other close branches of photography (such as documentary photography, street photography or celebrity photography) by the qualities of:

- *Timeliness*: the images have meaning in the context of a published chronological record of events.
- *Objectivity*: the situation implied by the images is a fair and accurate representation of the events they depict.

— *Narrative*: the images combine with other news elements, to inform and give insight to the viewer or reader.

Unlike a reporter, who may gather information while far from the subject or after an event occurs, the photojournalist must make decisions instantly and carry a camera under the same circumstances as those involved in the subject (fire, war, rioting) - often while being exposed to the same risks. Photojournalism as a descriptive term often implies the use of a certain bluntness of style or approach to image-making - one would not call a normal wedding photographer a 'photojournalist', even though they cover a timely event and their images may be published in the press.

Photojournalism has been a major element of newspaper and magazine reporting since the early twentieth century, although its historic origins have been traced to mid 19th century European battlefield photography by British press reporters in the Crimean War. Its use was greatly spurred by the development of the commercial 35mm Leica camera.

In the "golden age" of photojournalism (1930s-1950s), some magazines, Picture Post (London), Paris Match (Paris), Life (USA), Sports Illustrated (USA)) and newspapers (The Daily Mirror (London), The Daily Graphic (New York)) built their huge readerships and reputations largely on their use of photography, and photographers such as Robert Capa, Alfred Eisenstaedt, Margaret Bourke-White, W. Eugene Smith became well-known names. In Migrant Mother Dorothea Lange produced the seminal image of the Great Depression. The FSA also employed several other photo journalists to document the depression.

Farm Security Administration

From 1935 to 1942, the Farm Security Administration and

its predecessor the Resettlement Administration were part of Franklin Roosevelt's New Deal, and were designed to address agricultural problems and rural poverty associated with the Great Depression. A special photographic section of the agency, headed by Roy Stryker, was intended merely to provide public relations for its programs, but instead produced what some consider one of the greatest collections of documentary photographs ever created in the USA. If such documentary photography can be called 'photojournalism' remains debatable, since the FSA photographers had much more time & resources to create their work than would usually be the case. They also had a wider brief.

World War II brought a tremendous increase in the supply and demand for quality photojournalism. In its latter stages, the war also stimulated the supply of new faster & smaller cameras from Japan to Europe and the USA. In 1947, two years after World War 2 ended, the Magnum Photos photographic agency was founded by four photographers: Robert Capa, Henri Cartier-Bresson, George Rodger, and David Seymour. Magnum differed from other agencies in that it was a co-operative (all members of the agency were also partial owners).

Magnum is still a highly respected photo-agency to this day and membership is extremely selective. There is a review process once a year during which portfolios from applicants are viewed by all current members. From there, the few who are invited to join must withstand a several year probationary period before they can be considered full members. Many probationary members are asked to leave after one or two years. Some of the most famous contemporary magnum photographers have left the agency for various reasons either to be independents or to begin their own agencies. Magnum Photos has more or less been experiencing financial troubles for the last 40 years.

Since the late 1970s, photojournalism and documentary photography have increasingly been accorded a place in art galleries alongside art photography. Luc Delahaye, Chin-Chi Chiang, both Magnum photographer to name a few among many exhibit in galleries regularly.

News organisations and journalism training schools run many different awards for photojournalists. Since 1968, Pulitzer Prizes have been awarded for the following categories of photojournalism: 'Feature Photography', 'Spot News Photography' and 'Capture the Moment'.

Photojournalism works within the same ethical approaches to objectivity that are applied by other journalists. What to shoot, how to frame and how to edit are constant considerations. Often, ethical conflicts can be mitigated or enhanced by the actions of a sub-editor or picture editor, who takes control of the images once they have been delivered to the news organisation. The photojournalist often has no say as to how images are ultimately used.

The emergence of digital photography offers whole new realms of opportunity for the manipulation, reproduction, and transmission of images. It has inevitably complicated many of the ethical issues involved. The U.S. National Press Photographers Association, and other professional organizations, maintain a Code of Ethics to address what are thought to be the proper approaches to these issues. Major ethical considerations are often enscribed - with more or less success - into law. The law on photography often varies greatly from nation to nation. The legal situation is further complicated when one considers that photojournalism made in one country will often be published in many other countries.

Impact of New Technologies

Smaller, lighter cameras greatly enhanced the role of the

photojournalist. Since the 1960s, motor-drives, electronic flash, auto-focus, better lenses and other camera enhancements have made their jobs easier. New digital cameras means that photojournalists are no longer limited by the length of a roll of film, as 1000s of images can be stored on a single microdrive or flash card. Content remains the most important element of photojournalism, but the ability to extend deadlines and compress the process of gathering and editing that content has changed greatly.

As recently as fifteen years ago, it took nearly thirty minutes to scan and transmit a single color photograph from a remote location to the news office for printing. Now, equipped with a digital camera, a mobile phone and a laptop computer, the print photojournalist can send a high quality image in seconds, only minutes after an event occurs. Video phones and portable satellite links increasingly allow for the mobile transmission of images from almost any point on the earth. There is some concern amongst news-photographers that photojournalism as a profession as it is known today may change to the degree that it is unrecognizable as image capturing technology naturally progresses. There is also concern that less and less print publications are commissioning serious photojournalism on timely issues.

Investigative journalism is a branch of journalism that usually concentrates on a very specific topic, and typically requires a lot of work to yield results. The classic example is the uncovering of the Watergate Scandal by Bob Woodward and Carl Bernstein, resulting in reports being published in the Washington Post. The exact definition tends to differ, although most definitions tend to include uncovering information that would be detrimental to someone else that was being hidden.

The 'Insight' team of "The Sunday Times" achieved great renown in the 1960s for its exposure of Public Health scandals, most notably Thalidomide. Paul Foot used his columns in "The Daily Mirror" and "Private Eye" to expose miscarriages of justice. Some of the means reporters can use for their fact-finding: studying neglected sources, such as archives, phone records, address books, tax records and license records.

Yellow Journalism

Yellow journalism is a term given to any widespread tendencies or practices within media organizations which are detrimental to, or substandard from the point of view of, journalistic integrity. "Yellow journalism" may for example refer to sensationalized news reporting that bears only a superficial resemblance to journalism. Journalistic professionalism, as now understood, is the supposed antidote. Instead of "yellow journalism", media bias is a commonly-used misnomer.

The term, as it commonly applies, refers to news organizations for whom sensationalism, profiteering, and in some cases propaganda and jingoism, take dominance over factual reporting. Most cases tend to be related to journalistic bias, and the endemic practices of particular organizations to operate as mouthpieces, for rather limited and particular allegiances, rather than for the public trust.

There is a very long history. Recent accusations of yellow journalism center around media infotainment and corporate media, referring to organizations where business interests supersede the interests of news organizations to accurately report damaging facts about influential corporations and common practices within corporate industry. In certain cases, the links between political, business, and media worlds, are alleged to violate various laws ranging from fraud to antitrust.

In the modern context of near-instant television news coverage, a perceived careless lack of fact-checking for the sake of a breaking news story might be refered to as 'yellow journalism'. Aspects of yellow journalism can vary at the minimum from the sporadic use of unnecessarily colorful adjectives, up to a systematic tendency to report falsehoods as fact.

The term has largely fallen into disuse as the media world has grown both in scope and in complexity. Further, because most media outlets have cultural allegiances or business practices which to one degree or other force them to deviate from idealized concepts of reporting, accusations of "yellow journalism" tend to be few. Print journalists have tended towards building a career reputation of consistent and thorough professionalism, to gain respect and prominence. News anchors, for example, may be chosen not for their skills at journalism, but rather for their presentation, appearance, and personality.

A current perceived rift is therefore more akin to a segmentation according to definitions of "news". The public still attaches to "news" the connotations of "journalism". Because of these developments, the common definition of "news" no longer belongs in the domain of journalists, but to wider television and internet media outlets over a vast spectrum of target issues and audiences. The proliferation of web media has in a certain sense re-validated journalistic ethics: reports that conform best tend to be treated as more authoritative.

"Pseudo-news" organizations draw general audiences, who tend fall into market demographics that each favor particular blends of issues-based entertainment along with their "news". Reputation and ethics do not necessarily coincide at all times. Well-established institutions such as the New York Times can be at fault. Many journalists find conflicts between their employment and their professionalism as journalists.

The sensationalized human-interest stories of the yellow press increased circulation and readership heavily throughout the 19th century, especially in the United States. Early practitioners, such as Joseph Pulitzer and William Randolph Hearst, seem to have equated the sensational reporting of murders, gory accidents, and the like, with the need of the democratic common man to be entertained by subjects beyond dry politics. Two early yellow newspapers were Pulitzer's New York World and Hearst's New York Journal American.

While most early newspapers tended toward expressing a viewpoint, the prototypical example of yellow journalism was the late 19th century Hearst Newspapers' consistent and deliberate falsification of whole incidents, claiming a humanitarian crisis among Cubans at the hands of Spanish troops. Hearst had personally written or directed the production of a number of sensational stories that exaggerated the claims of Spanish cruelty toward their Cuban subjects. The stories, combining both a sense of urgency and moral outrage, were wildly popular, and Hearst directed his papers to market and exploit this trend to the fullest.

Having been successful not only in convincing the public for the cause for war, Hearst had managed to sway the political vote as well. This reporting sparked a public outcry that led to the Spanish-American War, wherin American intervention proved to be disastrous. Americans would soon find themselves occupying both Cuba and the Philippines, and Hearst found himself courted by politicians seeking his powers of influence.

The viewing of motion pictures appears continuous only because of the slow response of the eye, optic nerves, and brain to changes (called persistence of vision). If your persistence was very short you would perceive a movie as a single frame picture, followed by black, followed by the next frame, etc. It is possible to view the black space between frames and the passing of the shutter by the following technique: Close your eyelids, then periodically rapidly blink open and closed. If done fast enough you will be able to randomly "trap" the image between frames, or during shutter motion. This will not work with television due to the persistence of the phosphors nor with LCD or DLP light projectors due to the continuity of image, although certain color artifacts may appear with some digital projection technologies.

An incandescent lamp or an electric arc light produces illuminating photons. The traditional carbon arc or modern xenon arc light source produces sufficient heat to burn the film should the film remain stationary for more than a fraction of a second. Xenons were introduced in the 1950s and are now the more common source, being easier and safer to maintain for the most part. A metal blade which cuts off light before it can get to the film - usually this is part of the lamphouse. Some projectors have both a manually controlled and electronically one each; the electronic one is used for changeovers.

Dousers protect the film when the lamp is on but the film is not moving, preventing the film from melting from prolonged exposure to the direct heat of the lamp. A curved reflector redirects light that would otherwise be wasted toward the condensing lens. A positive curvature lens concentrates the reflected and direct light toward the film gate. A single image of the series of images comprising the movie is positioned and held flat within an aperture called the gate. The gate also provides a slight amount of friction so that the film does not advance or retreat except when driven to advance the film to the next image.

A rotating petal or gated cylindrical shutter interrupts the emitted light during the time the film is advanced to the next frame. Modern shutters are designed with a flicker-rate of two or even sometimes three times the frame rate of the film, so as to reduce the perception of screen flickering. A lens system with multiple optical elements directs the image of the film to a viewing screen. Different lenses are used for different aspect ratios. Each of these lenses comes with an aperture plate, a piece of metal with a precisely cut rectangular hole in the middle of equivalent aspect ratio. The aperture plate is placed just behind the gate, and masks off any light from hitting the image outside of the area intended to be shown.

Viewing Screen

In most cases this is a reflective surface which may be either aluminized (for high contrast in moderate ambient light) or a white surface with small glass beads (for high brilliance under dark conditions). In a commercial theater, the screen also has hundreds of small, evenly spaced holes in order to allow the passage of air to and from the speakers and subwoofer which often are directly behind it.

Two Reel System

The two reel system is also known as a changeover system, after the switching mechanism that operates between the end of one reel and the beginning of the next. In a two reel system the feed reel has a slight drag to maintain tensioning in the film, while the takeup reel is driven with a constant tension by a mechanism that is allowed to slip. The two reel system was almost universally used before the advent of the single reel system for movie theaters in order to be able to show feature-length films. Although one reel long-play systems tend to be more popular with the newer multiplexes, the two reel system is still in significant use to this day.

The projector operator operates two projectors, threading one with the next reel while the other projector plays the current reel. As the current reel approaches its end, the projectionist looks for cues, also known as cigarette burns, at the upper right corner of the picture. Usually these are dots or circles, although they can also be slashes. The first cue appears twelve feet (3.7 m) or eight seconds at 24 frame/s before the end of the reel, and signals the projectionist to start the motor of the projector containing the next reel. After another ten and a half feet (3.2 m) or seven seconds at 24 frame/s, the changeover cue should appear, which signals the projectionist to actually make the changeover.

When this second cue appears, the projectionist has one and a half feet (457 mm) or one second at 24 frame/s to make the changeover - if it doesn't occur within one second, the tail black leader of the exhausted reel will be projected on the screen. On some projectors, the operator would be alerted to the change by a bell that operated when the feed reel rotation exceeded a certain speed, although many such projectors do not have such an auditory system. During the actual operation of a changeover, the two projectors use an interconnected electrical control connected to the changeover button so that as soon as the button is pressed, the douser on the old reel is closed in sync with the douser for the new reel.

If done properly, a changeover should be virtually unnoticeable to an audience. In older theaters, there may be manually operated, sliding covers in front of the projection booth's windows. A changeover with this system is often clearly visible as a wipe on the screen. The size of the reels can vary based on the projectors, but generally films are divided and distributed in reels of roughly 2000 feet (610 m) about 22 minutes at 24 frame/s. Some projectors can even accommodate up to 6000 feet (1,830 m), which minimizes the number of changeovers in a showing. Certain countries also divide their film reels up differently; Russian films, for example, often come on 1000 foot (305 m) reels, although it's likely that most projectionists working with changeovers would combine them into longer reels of at least 2000 feet (610 m), to minimize changeovers and also give sufficient time for threading and any possibly needed troubleshooting time.

There are two largely used single reel systems (also known as long-play systems) today: the tower system (vertical feed and takeup) and the platter system (horizontal feed and takeup). The tower system largely resembles the two reel system, except in that the tower itself is generally a separate piece of equipment used with a slightly modified standard projector. The feed and takeup reels are held vertically on the axis, except behind the projector, on oversized spools with 12,000 foot (3,660 m) capacity or about 133 minutes at 24 frame/s. This large capacity alleviates the need for a changeover on an average-length feature; all of the reels are spliced together into one giant one.

The tower is designed with four spools, two on each side, each with its own motor. This allows the whole spool to be immediately rewound after a showing; the extra two spools on the other side allow for a film to be shown while another is being rewound or even made up directly onto the tower. Each spool requires its own motor in order to set proper tensioning for the film, since it has to travel (relatively) much further between the projector film transport and the spools. As each spool gains or loses film, the tension must be periodically checked and adjusted so that the film can be transported on and off the spools without either sagging or snapping.

In a platter system the individual 20 minute reels of film are also spliced together as one large reel, but the film is then wound onto a horizontal rotating table called a platter. Three or more platters are stacked together to create a platter system. Most of the platters in a platter system will be occupied by film prints; whichever platter happens to be empty serves as the "take-up reel" to receive the film that is playing from another platter. The way the film is fed from the platter to the projector is not unlike an eight-track audio cartridge.

Film is unwound from the center of the platter through a mechanism called a "brain" which controls the speed of the platter's rotation so that it matches the speed of the film as it is fed to the projector. The film winds through a series of rollers from the platter stack to the projector, through the projector, through another series of rollers back to the platter stack, and then onto the platter serving as the take-up reel. This system makes it possible to project a film several times a day without needing to rewind it. As the projectionist threads the projector for each showing, he transfers the brain mechanism from the empty platter to the full platter and the film then plays back onto the platter it came from.

In the case of a double feature, each film plays from a full platter onto an empty platter, swapping positions on the platter stack throughout the day. The advantage of a platter is that the film isn't subjected to the stresses of being rewound each show. Rewinding risks rubbing the film against itself, which can cause scratching of the film and smearing of the emulsion which carries the pictures. The disadvantages of the platter system are that the film can acquire diagonal scratches on it if proper care is not taken while threading film from platter to projector, and the film has more opportunity to collect dust and dirt as long lengths of film are exposed to the air. A clean projection booth kept at the proper humidity is of great importance, as are cleaning devices that can remove dirt from the film print as it plays.

The single reel system can allow for the complete automation of the projection booth operations, given the proper auxiliary equipment. Since films are still transported in multiple reels they must be joined together when placed on the projector reel and taken apart when the film is to be returned to the distributor. It is the complete automation that has enabled the modern "multiplex" cinema - a single site typically containing from 16 to 24 theaters with only a few projection and sound technicians, rather than a platoon of projectionists. The multiplex also offers a great amount of flexibility to a theater operator, enabling multiple theaters to exhibit the same popular production in multiple theaters with staggered starting times.

Smooth wheels with triangular pins called sprockets engage perforations punched into one or both edges of the film stock. These serve to set the pace of film movement through the projector and any associated sound playback system.

As with motion picture cameras, the intermittent motion of the gate requires that there be loops above and below the gate in order to serve as a buffer between the constant speed enforced by the sprockets above and below the gate and the intermittent motion enforced at the gate. Some projectors also have a sensitive trip pin above the gate to guard against the upper loop becoming too big. If the loop hits the pin, it will close the dousers and stop the motor to prevent an excessively large loop from jamming the projector.

A spring loaded pressure plate functions to align the film in a consistent image plane, both flat and perpendicular to the optical axis. It also provides sufficient drag to prevent film motion during the frame display, while still allowing free motion under control of the intermittent mechanism. The plate also has spring-loaded runners to help hold film while in place and advance it during motion.

For smaller gauge projectors (8mm and 16 mm), a pawl mechanism engages the film's sprocket hole one side, or holes on each side. This pawl advances only when the film is to be moved to the next image. As the pawl retreats for the next cycle it is drawn back and does not engage the film. This is similar to the claw mechanism in a motion picture camera. In 35 mm and 70 mm projectors, there usually is a special sprocket immediately underneath the pressure plate known as the intermittent sprocket.

Unlike the all the other sprockets in the projector, which run continuously, the intermittent sprocket operates in tandem with the shutter, and only moves while the shutter is blocking the lamp, so that the motion of the film cannot be seen. IMAX projectors use what's known as the rolling loop method, in which each frame is sucked into the gate by a vacuum, and positioned by registration pins in the perforations corresponding to that frame.

Projectors

Projectors are classified by the size of the film used. Typical film sizes:

8 mm: Long used for home movies before the video camera, this uses double sprocketed 16 mm film, which is run through the camera twice. The 16 mm film is then split lengthwise into two 8 mm pieces that are sliced to make a single projectable film with sprockets on one side.

Super 8: Developed by Kodak this film stock uses very small sprocket holes close to the edge that allow more of the film stock to be used for the images. This increases the quality of the image. The film is premade in the 8 mm width, not split during processing as is the earlier 8 mm. Magnetic stripes could be added to carry encoded sound to be added after film development.

16 mm: This was a popular format for audio-visual use in schools and as a high-end home entertainment system before the advent of broadcast television. It is also the smallest format that can carry an optically encoded sound track.

35 mm: The most common film size for theatrical productions during the first half of the 20th century. In fact, the common 35 mm camera, developed by Leica was designed to use this film stock and was originally intended to be used for test shots by movie directors and cinematographers.

70 mm: High end movie productions are often shot using this size and some theaters are capable of projecting it. 70 mm film is also used in both the flat and domed IMAX projection system. In IMAX the film is oriented for even more effective image area than in other formats.

Some high quality productions intended for 35 mm anamorphic release are shot in and the master prints constructed using 70 mm film stock. A 35 mm print made from a 70 mm master print is significantly better in appearance than an all 35 mm process.

Regardless of the sound format, any sound represented on the film image itself will not be the sound for the particular frame it occupies. All optical sound formats must be offset from the image because the image is projected with intermittent motion. If the sound head on the projector was adjacent to the gate, the sound would be a jerky start-stop-start-stop and so on. Therefore the sound head requires continuous motion and will be located a certain number of frames before or after the gate.

With 16 mm and the larger sizes it is practical to add a narrow channel of optically encoded sound track. This is read using an illuminating light or laser and a photo-sensor solar cell. In 16 mm, this is a single mono track, and the sound head is 26 frames after the gate. In 35 mm, this can be mono or stereo, the latter including several different Dolby sound matrixing systems (including Dolby A and Dolby SR). The sound head is located twenty frames after the gate for 35 mm projectors.

Originally optical sound was variable density, where the transparency/opacity level of the sound track was used to represent sound. This had disadvantages because the grain of the fill caused a background hiss, and so was replaced with the now-universal standard variable area. In this system, a clear waveform on black background represents the sound, and the width of the waveform is equivalent to the amplitude. Variable area does have slightly less frequency response than variable density, it should be noted.

Modern theatrical systems use optical representations of digitally encoded multi-channel sound. An advantage of digital systems is that the offset between the sound and picture heads can be varied and then set with the digital processors. Digital sound heads are usually above the gate. All digital sound systems currently in use have the ability to instantly and virtually imperceptibly fall back to the optical sound system should the digital data be corrupt or the whole system fail.

Cinema Digital Sound (CDS)

Created by Kodak and ORC (Optical Radiation Corporation), Cinema Digital Sound was the first attempt to bring multi-channel digital sound to first-run theaters. CDS was available on both 35 mm and 70 mm films. Film prints equipped with CDS did not have the conventional analog optical or magnetic soundtracks to serve as a "back-up" in case the digital sound was unreadable. Another disadvantage of not having an analog back-up track is that CDS required extra film prints be made for the theaters equipped to play CDS.

The three formats that followed, Dolby Digital, DTS and SDDS, can co-exist with each other and the analog optical soundtrack on a single version of the film print. This means that a film print carrying all three of these formats (and the analog optical format, usually Dolby SR) can be played in whichever format the theater is equipped to handle. CDS did not achieve wide-spread use and ultimately failed.

Sony Dynamic Digital Stereo (SDDS)

SDDS sound runs on the outside of 35 mm film, between the perforations and the edges, on both edges of the film. It is the only digital system that can handle up to eight tracks of sound. The additional two tracks are for an extra pair of screen channels (Left Center and Right Center) located between the 3 regular screen channels (Left, Center and Right). A pair of CCD's located in a unit above the projector read the two SDDS tracks. The information is decoded and decompressed before being passed along to a Sony cinema sound processor, which means it can be equalized in the digital domain.

In contrast, DTS and Dolby Digital soundtracks both are passed through to standard analog Dolby cinema sound processors which are also used for analog optical sound, so equalization of the sound is only analog. The digital compression of SDDS is better than DTS, but inferior to Dolby Digital. SDDS premiered with the film The Last Action Hero.

Also known to enthusiasts as Spectral Recording Digital or "SR-D." Sound is printed between the perforations and is 26 frames before the picture (the offset can be varied based on processing presets). It can handle up to six tracks, and has the best compression of the digital formats. The images between each perforation are read by a CCD located either above the projector or in the regular analog sound head below the film gate.

The information is then decoded, decompressed, and converted to analog by an SR-D processor before going to a standard Dolby analog multi-format cinema sound processor. A consumer version of Dolby Digital is also used on most DVD's, often at higher data rates than the original film.

Digital Theater Systems (DTS)

DTS actually stores the sound information on separate CD-ROMs supplied with the film. The CDs are fed into a special modified computer (usually a 386 or 486 system) which syncs up with the film through the use of DTS time code, decompresses the sound, and passes it through to a standard analog Dolby processor. The time code is placed between the optical sound tracks and the actual picture, and is read by an optical LED ahead of the gate. The time code is actually the only sound system which is not offset within the film from the picture, but still needs to be physically set offset ahead of the gate in order to maintain continuous motion.

Each disc can hold slightly over two hours of sound, so longer films will require a second disc, which means that the sound will temporarily revert back to the optical track while changing discs. DTS is a six track system (although it has an earlier, discontinued four track counterpart), and as might be expected of the oldest of the three digital systems, has the most inferior compression. Of the three digital formats currently in use, DTS is the only one that has been used with 70 mm presentations. DTS was premiered on Jurassic Park. A consumer version of DTS is available on some DVD's.

70 mm, which had no optical sound, used the 5 millimeters gained between the 65 mm negative and the final release print to place three magnetic tracks on each side of the perforations, for a total of six tracks. Unlike all other non-double head magnetic sound, 70 mm magnetic heads are located before the gate. Until the introduction of digital sound, it was fairly common for 35 mm films to

be blown up to 70 mm often just to take advantage of the greater number of sound tracks. 35 mm four-track magnetic sound was used from the 1950s through the mid 1970s for big-budget feature prints.

It was of excellent quality, although somewhat prone to damage and erasure over time. As analog optical stereo gained popularity (it was also more durable and far less expensive to include on a film print), 35 mm four-track magnetic sound was increasingly only used for special road show screenings, and the development of digital sound systems made it completely obsolete. 35 mm and 16 mm each are sometimes run in sync with a separate reel of magnetic sound; the image goes through a gate while the magnetic reel passes over a sound head.

Since the sound is on a separate reel, it does not need to be offset from the image. This system is usually used only for very low-budget or student productions, or for screening rough cuts of films before the creation of a final married print. Sync between the two reels is checked with SMPTE Academy leader, also known as countdown leader. If the two reels are synced, there should be one frame of "plop" sound exactly on the "3" frame of the countdown.On certain stocks of Super 8 and 16 mm it an iron-oxide sound recording strip was added for the direct synchronous recording of sound which could then be played by projectors with a magnetic sound head. It has since been discontinued by Kodak on both gauges.

Lenses and Screens

Before the advent of certain wide screen technologies, lenses always reproduced the exact proportions of the film image onto the screen. Such lenses are relatively simple to design and manufacture. Prior to modern wide screen, the industry standard image ratio of width to height was 4:3. 35 mm VistaVision was a wide screen orthographic system. The wide image was obtained by running the film horizontally across the gate so that the width limitation of the film was transformed to a height limitation.

The 1950's saw the development of wide screen films using special lenses for filming and projection. The images on these films retained the same proportions as in the earlier films (a 4:3 width to height ratio). The wide image is compressed onto the film in the camera using additional cylindrical elements within the lens, with a corresponding lens used in the projector to expand the image to the wide screen. This technique is called anamorphic projection and various implementations have been marketed under several brand names, including CinemaScope, Panavision and Superscope, with Technirama implementing a slightly different anamorphic technique using vertical expansion to the film rather than horizontal compression.

Of the anamorphic methods, arguably the best image was produced by the Todd-AO (for Michael Todd and American Optical) using 70 mm film and a large, curved screen. Around the World in Eighty Days starring David Niven and Cantinflas was the leading general release production using this process. A popular film recently released as a remake, the original was also released as a Cinemascope print, by comparison to the Todd-AO original as watching television is to being in a movie theater. Similar 70 mm processes include Super (and Ultra) Panavision and VistaVision.

The IMAX® dome projection method (called "OMNIMAX®") uses 70 mm film oriented to maximize the image area and extreme wide angle lenses to obtain an almost hemispherical image. The field of view is tilted, as is the projection hemisphere, so one may view a portion of the ground in the foreground. Owing to the great area covered by the picture it is not as bright as seen with flat screen projection, but the immersive qualities are quite convincing. While there are not many theaters capable of displaying this format there are regular productions in the fields of nature, travel, science, and history, and productions may be viewed in most U.S. large urban regions. These dome theaters are mostly located in large and prosperous science and technology museums.

The IMAX® flat screen system uses large format film, a wide and deep screen, and close and quite steep "stadium" seating. The effect is to fill the visual field to a greater degree than is possible with conventional wide screen systems. Like the IMAX® dome, this is found in major urban areas, but unlike the dome system it is practical to reformat existing movie releases to this method. Also, the geometry of the theater and screen are more amenable to inclusion within a newly constructed but otherwise conventional multiple theater complex than is the dome style theater.

One wide screen development during the 1950's used non-anamorphic projection, but used three side by side synchronised projectors. Called Cinerama, the images were projected onto an extremely wide, curved screen. Some seams were said to be visible between the images but the almost complete filling of the visual field made up for this. This showed some commercial success as a limited location (only in major cities) exhibition of the technology in This is Cinerama, but the only memorable story-telling film of two made for this technology was How the West Was Won, widely seen only in its Cinemascope re-release.

While neither a technical nor a commercial success, the business model survives as implemented by the documentary production, limited release locations, and long running exhibitions of IMAX® dome movies. A slide projector is an opto-mechanical device to view photographic slides. It has four main elements: a fan-cooled electric light bulb or other light source, a reflector and "condensing" lens to direct the light to the slide, a holder for the slide and a focusing lens. Light passes through the transparent slide and lens, and the resulting image is enlarged and projected onto a perpendicular flat screen so the audience can view its reflection. Alternatively the image may be projected onto a translucent "rear projection" screen, often used for continuous automatic display for close viewing.

The resolution and color brilliance of good quality 35mm slides (especially Kodachrome) projected onto a high quality screen far exceed that of modern in-home video. Common in the 1950s and 1960s households as an alternate to television or movie entertainment, family members and friends would gather, darken the living room and show slides of recent holidays or vacations, an often boring affair that incited heckling, catcalls and sleep. In-home photographic slides and slide projectors have largely been replaced by low cost paper prints, digital cameras, DVD media, video display monitors and digital projectors.

Stock photography is photography or other imagery of common landmarks, concepts, and events that can be used and reused for commercial design purposes. Book publishers, specialty publishers, magazines, advertising agencies, film makers, web designers, graphic artists, interior decor firms, corporate creative groups, and other entities utilize stock photography to fulfill the needs of their creative assignments. By using stock photography instead of hiring a photographer to perform on location shooting, customers can save valuable time and stay on budget.

With a wealth of images, stock photography databases that may be searched online save photo researchers valuable time when they are looking for just the right image. With today's digital delivery methods, images may be purchased online and delivered via FTP or email, the very same day. Stock photography is sometimes called a photo archive, or just stock photos. The term photo archive often refers to the website or physical location where the photographs are stored. Photo archives are also sometimes called image banks. As modern stock photography distributors often carry stills, video, and illustrations, none of the existing terminology provides a perfect match for the state of the industry.

Images are filed at an agency that negotiates licensing fees on the photographer's behalf in exchange for a percentage, or in some cases owns the images outright. Pricing is determined by size of audience or readership, how long the image is to be used, country or region where the images will be used and whether royalties are due to the image creator or owner. Often, an image can be licensed for less than $200. The client may, however, request an "exclusive", preventing other customers from using the same image for a specified length of time. Such sales can command many thousands of dollars, both because they tend to be high-exposure and because the agency is gambling that the image would not have made more money had it remained in circulation.

"Exclusive" photos are often referred to as rights managed. Photos that do not allow for an exclusive purchase are often referred to as royalty free. Some stock photography sites offer low-resolution photography free for the purpose of preparing advertising comps to demonstrate a design. If the advertiser decides to use the image, the rights to use the high-resolution image then can be negotiated.

One of the first major stock photography agencies was the one founded in 1920 by H. Armstrong Roberts, which continues today under the name Retrofile. For many years, stock photography consisted largely of outtakes ("seconds") from commercial magazine assignments. By the 1980s, it had become a specialty in its own right, with photographers creating new material for the express purpose of submitting it to a stock house. Agencies attempted to become more sophisticated about following and anticipating the needs of advertisers and communicating these needs to photographers.

Photographs were composed with more of an eye for how they might look when combined with other elements; for example, a photo might be shot vertically with space at the top and down the left side, with the conscious intention that it might be licensed for use as a magazine cover. Leading agencies during this time included The Image Bank, Comstock Images, FPG, and Masterfile. In the 1990s, a period of consolidation followed, with Getty Images and Corbis becoming the two largest companies as a result of acquisitions. Today, stock photography companies have largely moved online.

2

Print Media

Printing is an industrial process for reproducing copies of texts and images, typically with ink on paper using a printing press. It is an essential part of publishing. Books are usually printed today using the technique of offset printing, and occasionally relief print. The largest commercial and industrial printer in the world is Montréal, Quebec based Quebecor World.

Printing was first discovered and developed in China. Primitive Woodblock printing was already in use by the 6th century BC. The oldest surviving book printed using the more sophisticated block printing dates from 868 AD. The movable type printer was invented by Pi Sheng in 1040. The movable type metal printing press was invented in Korea between 1234 and 1241. By the 12th and 13th century many Arabic and Chinese libraries contained tens of thousands of printed books. There is little direct evidence, but it is highly probable that Chinese printing technology diffused into Europe through trade links that went through India and on through the Arabic world.

Johann Gutenberg, of the German city of Mainz, developed European printing technology in 1440. Basing the design of his machine on a wine press, Gutenberg developed the use of raised and movable type and from the start used oil based inks. This development of the printing press revolutionized the spread of knowledge: a printing press was built in Venice in 1469, and the city had 417 printers by 1500. In 1476, a printing press was developed in England by William Caxton; in 1539, the Italian Juan Pablos set up an imported press in Mexico City, Mexico. Stephen Day built the first printing press in North America at Massachusetts Bay in 1628, and helped establish the Cambridge Press.

In Prints and Visual Communication, William Ivins offers the following concise history of a series of rapid innovations in image and type printing at the end of the eighteenth century:

> At the end of the eighteenth century there were several remarkable innovations in the graphic techniques and those that were utilized to make their materials. Bewick developed the method of using engraving tools on the end of the wood. Senefelder discovered lithography. Blake made relief etchings. Early in the nineteenth century Stanhope, George E. Clymer, Koenig and others introduced new kinds of type presses, which for strength surpassed anything that had previously been known.

Computer Printing

A document can also be printed by a laser printer, inkjet, or other computer printer. In recent years, computer printing and industrial printing processes have converged, leading to the development of digital printing and on-demand printing. Letterpress printing is the oldest printing technique, in which a raised surface is inked and then pressed against a smooth substance to obtain an image in reverse. Early Chinese wood-blocks used characters or images carved in relief, and this form of image printing was known in Europe in the 13th century.

In the 1400s, Johann Gutenberg is credited with the invention of printing from individually-cast, reusable letters set together in a forme. He used a wooden press where the type surface was inked and paper laid carefully on top by hand, then slid under a padded surface and pressure applied from above by a huge threaded screw. Later metal presses used a knuckle and lever arrangement instead of the screw, but the principle was the same. With the advent of industrial mechanisation, the inking was carried out by rollers which would pass over the face of the type and move out of the way onto a separate ink-bed where they would pick up a fresh film of ink for the following sheet. Meanwhile a sheet of paper was slid against a hinged platen which was then rapidly pressed onto the type and swung back again to have the sheet removed and the next sheet inserted.

In a fully-automated 20th century press, the paper was fed and removed by vacuum sucker grips. Rotary presses were used for high-speed work. In the oscillating press, the forme slid under a drum around which each sheet of paper got wrapped for the impression, sliding back under the inking rollers while the paper was removed and a new sheet inserted. In a newspaper press, a papier-mâché mixture (flong) was used to make a mould of the entire forme of type, then dried and bent, and a curved metal plate cast against it.

The plates were clipped to a rotating drum, and could thus print against a continuous reel of paper at the enormously high speeds required for overnight newspaper production. As computerised typesetting and imaging replaced cast metal types, letterpress began to die out, as photographic imaging onto smooth flexible plates became more economical. A small amount of high-quality art and hobby metal letterpress printing remains—fine letterpress work is crisper than offset litho because a microscopic border of ink is squashed out around each letter, giving greater visual definition. There is however still a large amount of flexographic printing, which uses rubber plates to print on curved or awkward surfaces, and a lesser amount of relief printing from huge wooden letters for lower-quality poster work.

Block printing is a form of printing first developed in China. The earliest known example with an actual date is a copy of the Diamond Sutra from 868 A.D, though the practice of block printing is probably about two thousand years old. The first step in block printing is the production of the original document. This is laid on a large, smooth wooden block and fixed into place, reversed. Next, craftsmen of various skill levels, ranging from master carvers for the fine work to less talented artisans for cheaper blocks or less important sections, carve the original painted, drawn or written image into the block of wood. The block can now be covered with ink and used in a press to create duplicates of the original.

In some ways block printing is superior to cast type or moveable type—for a language such as Chinese which has a very broad character set, block prints are much cheaper to produce for the initial run. The process also allows greater artistic freedom, such as the easy inclusion of pictures and diagrams. However, printing blocks are not very durable, and deteriorate very rapidly with use, requiring constant replacement which limits the possibility of large-scale print runs. Flexography, normally abbreviated to flexo, is a method of printing most commonly used for packaging.

A flexo print is achieved by creating a mirrored master of the required image as a 3D relief in a rubber or polymer material—compare with children's potato printing. A measured amount of ink is deposited upon the surface of the printing plate using an anilox roll. The print surface then rotates, contacting the print material which transfers the ink. Flexo is so named because it was originally used as a method of printing onto corrugated cardboard which has a very uneven surface. It is required that the printing plate surface maintain contact with the cardboard, which it does by being a flexible. Also unprinted high points on the cardboard must not get printed by ink remnants not on the plate surface, which is achieved by ensuring a sufficient depth for the non-print areas of the plate.

Originally flexo printing was very crude. Over the last few decades great strides have been taken in improvements to the plate material and the method of plate creation - usually photographic exposure followed by chemical etch, but also by direct laser engraving. Full colour picture printing is now possible. Flexo has an advantage over lithography in that it can use a wider range of inks and is good at printing on a variety of different materials. Typical product printed this way includes: 'brown' cardboard boxes, cornflake packets, crisp packets, yoghurt pot tops,

Intaglio printing is frequently used in the production of currency. Intaglio is a printmaking technique in which the image is incised into a surface. Normally, copper or zinc plates are used as a surface, and the incisions are created by etching, engraving, drypoint, or mezzotint. Collographs may also be printed as intaglio plates. To print an intaglio plate, the surface is covered in ink, and then rubbed vigorously with tarlatan cloth or newspaper to remove the ink from the surface, leaving it only in the incisions. A damp piece of paper is placed on top, and the plate and paper are run through a printing press that, through pressure, transfers the ink from the recesses of the plate to the paper.

The term is sometimes also used for engraved seals, which leave a raised design when pressed on to the material to be stamped, and is an Italian word that means the activity of carving (mainly) wood for decorative purposes.

Lithography

Lithography was invented by Alois Senefelder in Bohemia in 1798, and it was the first new printing process since the invention of relief printing in the fifteenth century. Lithography is a method for printing on a smooth surface, as well as a method of manufacturing semiconductor and MEMS devices. Lithography as a manual process is based on the repulsion of oil and water. The image is placed on the surface with an oil-based medium; acid is then used to 'burn' the oil into the surface. When printing, the surface is covered in water, which remains on the non-oily surface and avoids the oily parts; a roller can then apply an oil-based ink that adheres only to the oily portion of the surface.

In the early days of lithography, a smooth piece of limestone was used. After the oil-based image was put on the surface, acid burned the image onto the surface; gum arabic, a water soluble solution, was then applied, sticking only to the non-oily surface and sealing it. During printing, water adhered to the gum arabic surfaces and avoided the oily parts, while the oily ink used for printing did the opposite. Within a few years of its invention, the lithographic process was used to create multi-colour printed images, a process known by the middle of the 19th Century as Chromolithography, and many fine examples of chromolithographic colour printing and publishing were achieved in America and Europe during this period. A separate stone was used for each colour, and the print went through the press separately for each stone. The main challenge was of course to keep the images in register.

Today, however, aluminum or plastic plates are used. The plates already have a brushed, or "roughened" texture, but they are covered with a smooth photosensitive emulsion. A photographic negative of the desired image is laid on top of the plate, and exposed to light, transferring a positive image to the emulsion. The emulsion is then chemically treated to remove the unexposed portions of the emulsion. The plate is affixed to a drum on a printing press, and water is rolled over the plate, which adheres to the rough, or negative portions of the image. A roller coated with ink is then rolled over the plate, which adheres to the smooth, or positive portions of the image. If this image were directly transferred to paper, it would create a positive image, but the paper would be moistened.

Instead, a drum covered with a rubber surface is rolled over the plate, which squeezes away the water, and picks up the ink. The drum is then rolled over the paper, transferring the ink. Because the image is first transferred to the rubber drum, the process is called "offset lithography," due to the fact that the image is offset to the drum before being applied to the paper. Many innovations and technical changes have occurred to this process over the years, including the development of presses that utilize several plates to build up a multi-color image in one pass through the press, and the Dahlgren inking system, which eliminates the separate moistening step.

At the input end, the advent of desktop publishing made it possible for almost anyone to quickly develop professional quality layouts, and the development of the imagesetter enabled print shops to skip the intermediate step of photographing a layout; they could now print directly from the computer to film. Since the start of the 21st century, the platesetter has eliminated film altogether by printing directly to the plate itself.

Semiconductor Lithography

Semiconductor lithography was developed for use in manufacturing microchips. It is also used in MEMS applications, as it is one of the best methods currently in use for manufacturing devices on scales much smaller than a micrometer. Although silicon lithographic technology is most advanced, other materials are also used. The emerging technology of a maskless lithography process for the semiconductor is also being used.

Lithography as an artistic medium

During the first twenty-five years of the nineteenth century, the practice of lithography was predominantly restricted to cheap reproductions of paintings and drawings. However, around 1825 the French artists Ingres, Géricault, and Delacroix embraced the process as a way to avoid the problems inherent in wood-block and copper engraving, namely, the near necessity of middlemen like draughtsmen and engravers.

The advantage to lithography was that he or she could draw or paint directly onto the lithographic material and avoid entirely the intermediate steps and craftsmen involved in engraving. Therefore, an artist's drawing and a lithographic print made from it were nearly identical - no reworking or transfer to another medium was necessary. It also afforded, at the time, the most complete range of line color from white to black. Goya's lithographs 'The Bulls of Bordeaux' and Delacroix's illustrations to Goethe's Faust were the groundbreaking "artist's lithographs" that sparked a flood of artists who dabbled in lithography, including Prud'hon, Cezanne, Manet, and, of course, its greatest practitioner, Daumier, whose prints began to appear in the 1830s.

For the first time in history, an artist was able to send out into the world his or her own drawing, not in unique specimen but in editions. Each impression had all their personality, skill, and genius, with no recourse to intermediary persons and technological steps. Offset printing is a widely used printing technique where the inked image is transferred first to a rubber blanket, then to the printing surface. When used in combination with the lithographic process, which is based on the repulsion of oil and water, the offset technique helps avoid the transfer of water to the printing surface along with the ink.

The advantages of offset printing include:

— Consistent high image quality—sharper and cleaner than letterpress because the rubber blanket conforms to the texture of the printing surface

— Usability on a wide range of printing surfaces in addition to smooth paper (e.g., wood, cloth, metal, leather, rough paper)

— Quick and easy production of printing plates

— Longer plate life than on direct litho presses—because there is no direct contact between the plate and the printing surface.

The first lithographic offset printing press was created in England around 1875 and was designed for printing on metal. The offset cylinder was covered with specially treated cardboard that transferred the printed image from the litho stone to the surface of the metal. About five years later, the cardboard covering of the offset cylinder was changed to rubber, which is still the most commonly used material.

The first person to use an offset press to print on paper was probably American Ira Washington Rubel in 1903. He got the idea accidentally by noticing that whenever a sheet of paper was not fed into his lithographic press during operation, the stone printed its image to the rubber-covered impression cylinder, and the next impression had an image on both sides: direct litho on the front and an image from the rubber blanket on the back. Rubel then noticed that the image on the back of the sheet was much sharper and clearer than the direct litho image because the soft rubber was able to press the image onto the paper better than the hard stone. He soon decided to build a press which printed every image from the plate to the blanket and then to the paper.

Brothers Charles and Albert Harris independently observed this process at about the same time and developed an offset press for the Harris Automatic Press Company soon after. Harris designed his offset press around a rotary letterpress machine. It used a metal plate bent around a cylinder at the top of the machine that pressed against ink and water rollers. A blanket cylinder was positioned directly below, and in contact with, the plate cylinder. The impression cylinder below pressed the paper to the blanket in order to transfer the image to the sheet. While this basic process is still used today, refinements include two-sided printing and web feeding.

During the 1950s, offset printing became the most popular form of commercial printing as improvements were made in plates, inks and paper, maximizing the technique's superior production speed and plate durability. Today, the majority of printing, including newspapers, is done by the offset process. Although offset printing is by far the most dominant form of commercial printing, "private or hobby presses," engaged in patient production of limited editions of fine quality books, often use letterpress as well as offset methods, some "purists" preferring the slightly embossed look resulting from the direct impression of inked type upon fine paper. These books are sometimes printed from hand-set foundry type.

Rotogravure Printing

Rotogravure, in shortly gravure, is a type of intaglio printing process, in that it involves engraving the image onto an image carrier. In gravure printing, the image is engraved onto a cylinder because, like offset and flexography, it is a rotary printing press. This means that gravure presses print on rolls of paper, rather than sheets of paper. Gravure cylinders nowadays are typically engraved digitally by a diamond tipped or laser tipped etching machine. On the gravure cylinder, the engraved image is composed of small recessed cells or 'dots' that act as tiny wells. Their depth and size control the amount of ink that gets transferred to the paper.

A rotogravure printing press has one printing unit for each color. The number of units vary depending on what colors are required to produce the final image. There are five basic components in each color unit: an engraved cylinder, the ink fountain, the doctor blade, the impression roller, and the dryer. While the press is in operation, the engraved cylinder is partially immersed in the ink fountain, filling the recessed cells. As the cylinder rotates, it draws ink out of the fountain with it. Acting as a squeegee, the doctor blade scrapes the cylinder before it makes contact with the paper, removing ink from the non-printing areas. Next, the paper gets sandwiched between the impression roller and the gravure cylinder. This is where the ink gets transferred from the recessed cells to the paper.

The purpose of the impression roller is to apply force, pressing the paper onto the gravure cylinder, ensuring even and maximum coverage of the ink. Then the paper goes through a dryer because it must be completely dry before going through the next color unit and absorbing another coat of ink. Security printing is the field of the printing industry that deals with the printing of items such as banknotes, passports, stock certificates, postage stamps and identity cards. The main goal of security printing is to prevent forgery or counterfeiting. A number of technical methods are used in the security printing industry.

- *Special paper:* Most banknotes are made of heavy paper, sometimes mixed with linen, cotton, or other textile fibres. Some countries including Romania, Mexico and Australia produce banknotes made from polymer, in order to improve wear and tear, and permit the inclusion of a small transparent window a few millimeters in size as a security feature that is very difficult to reproduce using common counterfeiting techniques.
- *Watermarks:* A watermark is a recognizable image or pattern in paper that appears lighter when viewed by transmitted light (or darker when viewed by reflected light, atop a dark background). A watermark is made by impressing a water coated metal stamp or dandy roll onto the paper during manufacturing. Watermarks were first introduced in Bologna, Italy in 1282; as well as their use in security printing, they have also been used by papermakers to identify their product.
- Intaglio printing
- Geometric lathe work
- Microprinting
- Color-changing inks
- Split ink fountains
- Holograms
- Security threads
- Magnetic ink
- Serial numbers
- Hidden marks and "mistakes"
- Anti-copying marks
- Copy-evident paper
- Fluorescent dyes
- Registration of features on both sides

3

Print Journalism

In print media students will have an opportunity to explore the processes involved in gathering and writing news, preparing an editorial, writing feature and sports stories, preparing effective photographs, and contrasting newspapers with magazines.

Foundational Objectives

The foundational objectives for Journalism Studies 20 are as follows. Students will:

— recognize and appreciate the role of journalism in contemporary society and in their personal lives

— recognize and explore the ways in which print and broadcast media create and present a message

— recognize and create the various forms, conventions, and styles of journalistic writing

— recognize the attributes of quality journalism and the legal, ethical, and moral issues which confront the free press

— develop the speaking, listening, reading, writing, viewing, and representing skills needed to create various print publications and broadcast productions.

Learning Objectives

Students will:

— recognize the importance for journalists of interviewing, researching, and reporting

— consider how print journalism has changed and evolved over the years

— recognize how pervasive information is in contemporary society

— recognize the role of news reporting in print media, especially newspapers

— recognize the basic formats used in newspapers

— use the inverted pyramid style of news writing

— write effective headlines

— evaluate the quality and reliability of various forms and examples of journalism.

The following suggestions are intended to form a bank of ideas from which teachers and students can draw in each section of this module.

Reporters have three key jobs—getting an idea for a new story, digging out the key information, and then writing or telling the story. Interviewing and effective listening are essential journalistic skills. To give students an idea of what is involved, introduce the following assignment. Have students generate several ideas for a story that is newsworthy to their school or community. Have students choose one idea and frame questions to show what they want to find out about the idea (rather than presenting personal biases).

Then, students can brainstorm possible sources that may be willing to answer their questions. Have students prepare their interview questions. Have them find a partner and practise asking the questions. They should revise their questions as needed and then conduct the interview(s). Have students double check their sources for accuracy and then write the news story. Directions for this process follow.

1. Brainstorm several ideas that might be newsworthy stories in your school or community. Journalists often begin with a question, a hunch, or an idea at the back of their minds that some issue, person, or event needs to be explored and documented. Choose one idea. Does the story idea display any of the following elements?

   — Importance (Is the news important to the lives of the readers?)

   — Timeliness (Are the events of interest to readers right now?)

   — Proximity (Did the events occur near the readers?)

   — Prominence (Are the people involved in the news well-known?)

   — Conflict (Are people opposing each other?)

   — Progress (Is the news about new developments?)

   — Emotions (Do the events involve feelings of love, hate, fear, pity, or horror?)

2. Frame questions to show what you want to find out (rather than documenting preconceived ideas).

3. Brainstorm possible sources that may be willing to answer your questions.

4. Prepare your interview questions. Begin your questions with who, what, when, where, why, how—words that signal you are a news writer.

5. Find a partner and practise asking the questions. Ask your partner to play the part of the interviewee.

Record the interview and take notes as you conduct the interview. Using only your notes, try writing a draft of the story and include several quotes. Then listen to the tape of the interview. Are the quotes accurate? What could you do to improve your interviewing and notetaking technique?

6. Revise any questions you think need to be reworded.
7. Conduct the interview(s).

— First and foremost, listen carefully and courteously.

— Have a notetaking system and take notes only on what you understand at the time. Tape the interview, when appropriate.

— Let yourself become engaged--interested in the source's ideas, arguments, and work.

— Be flexible and prepared to change the direction of your interview.

— If you do not understand something, ask for an explanation.

— Try to remain neutral in your demeanour--your body language, tone, and dress.

— Be careful with your questions--try to avoid loaded, leading, and closed questions.

— Do not get drawn into an argument.

— Use silence to your advantage.

8. Double check your sources for accuracy. Verify your facts. Call back. A professional reporter tries to find more than one source of information. Consider, for example, the following:

— what you saw or heard

— your interview with one or more participants or eyewitnesses

— other sources including reliable local media, reference books, almanacs, electronic databases, information services, etc.

9. Draft the story. Use the inverted pyramid with your lead paragraph answering the essential who, what, when, where, and why questions. Further important facts can be given in the middle paragraph.

10. Revise. Create a headline that encapsulates the story. If appropriate, include a photograph with a caption that is faithful to the story.

Have students study a variety of different types of newspapers. Have them consider the following:

1. List the different components of the papers. How are the components organized? What is common? What is different? Why?

2. What items make news? What makes these items newsworthy? How do readers know where to look for certain items? How is a weekly newspaper different from a daily? How is a tabloid different from a broadsheet? What is the size of the typical "newshole" (e.g., 40%)?

3. What are the typical elements of an editorial page? How does it differ from the front page? What is the opinion of the editorial? What signals are given to the reader that the editorial emphasizes opinion and comment rather than facts? Who stands to benefit from the opinion expressed? Who stands to lose? What facts does the editorial writer use to support the opinion? How does the writer attempt to persuade readers? Who owns the newspaper? How might this affect the content and viewpoints of the editorial page?

4. What role was played by pictures, headlines, and graphic treatments? What makes one paper more appealing than another?

5. What percentage of each paper is made up of advertising? Who is advertising? What advertiser dominates?
6. What sections of the newspaper appeal to you? What sections do you read first? What do you skip? Why? What items would appeal most to teens? To adults? What can be deduced about the intended audience of the newspaper? What does the function of the paper appear to be?
7. Brainstorm "spin off" ideas that could stem from one news story in one of the papers. Consider the following categories: What "slant" could be put on each of these "spin off" ideas?

Truth and Accuracy

News is conveyed by letter, word or mouth And comes to us from North, East, West and South (Witt's Recreation). The letters N E W S used to be prefixed to newspapers to show that they obtained information from the four quarters of the world, and the supposition that our word news is thence derived is an ingenious conceit but destroyed by the old spelling newes; it is from the French nouvelles. Whatever the source or media, reporting what happened in plain, clear language is the goal of a good news reporter. As students work through this module, they should read the news in newspapers and magazines, watch TV news reports, and listen to radio news. Then, they should try their hand at writing a good news story.

Learning Objectives

Students will:

— recognize the importance for journalists of interviewing, researching, and reporting

— evaluate the quality and reliability of various forms and examples of journalism
— recognize what is news
— recognize the elements of a news story
— distinguish fact from opinion
— understand effective news gathering and editing techniques
— use the inverted pyramid style of news writing
— write various types of news story leads and news stories
— quote accurately, paraphrase where appropriate, and use appropriate attribution methods
— recognize the differences between a news story and sports writing
— write clear, informative sports stories
— write effective headlines
— understand the purpose of a news release
— understand the role of a news bureau
— use a journalism style guide.

Suggested activities

— With a partner, have students name as many news sources as they can for each of the media listed below:

Radio News	e.g., The World at Six
Television News	e.g., The National
Newspapers	e.g., The Globe and Mail
Magazines	e.g., Maclean's
Internet	e.g., www.cnn.com

— Which news source(s) do they prefer? Why? How often do they use the various sources to get news? What are the advantages and disadvantages of each source? What are the advantages of getting news from more than one source? Conversely, what is the danger of relying on one source?

— What is news? Of all the different kinds of information you find in a newspaper, which ones can be called "news"? Ask students to consider how they would describe the difference between "news" and "not news?" Do these distinctions blur in some articles? Journalists use different criteria to determine what is news. One approach is labelled the "Who cares?" method--assessing how much reader interest a story has. Another approach determines the news story's importance against criteria such as timeliness, proximity, human interest, conflict, prominence, and consequence. Have students summarize ten of their news stories and then survey a group of peers or members of their community, asking those surveyed to rate the stories in order of importance. Is there a general agreement? What does this tell us? Students can write their conclusions in their journals.

— With a partner, have students clip all the news stories from a recent daily newspaper. They can classify each according to type. They might consider: international news, national news, provincial news, municipal news, local news, political news, news about accidents or disasters, human interest news, news about famous people, news about wars or battles, sports news, crime news, news about finance and economics, business news, environmental news, science news, health and medicine news, education news, entertainment news, etc.

— Have students examine several news stories with a summary lead and inverted pyramid style of writing.

Have them identify the who, what, when, where, why, and how in each story. Which elements are introduced first? Why? Which ones appear in the lead? Which ones are saved for subsequent paragraphs? Why? Are people's names in the lead? Why or why not? How is the time element handled by the writer? Will the story still be newsworthy tomorrow or next week? Are reporters by-lines used? What kind of stories are usually by-lined?

— Have students compare a television newscast and a newspaper story from the same date. They can examine the lead, the length of the story, and the way quotes are used, and then write leads for the same story for a newspaper and television broadcast.

— Have students write a summary lead and inverted pyramid style story. They could listen to a short story, fairy tale, or narrative poem; take notes; identify the six main elements; and determine the information that is most important. After checking the spelling of names and quoting correctly, they could compare results with peers. What elements were placed in the lead? Why? What facts have been included or left out?

— Reporters can slant their stories by using loaded words, while editors can influence the readers' perceptions by the use of headlines, pictures, and juxtapositioning. Have students examine a hard news story and an editorial. Ask them to identify examples of fact, opinion, and bias in each. Ask students to read the section on sports reporting in the Canadian Press (CP) Style Book, and then determine what phrases may be used in a crime report, a council report, a "soft" newsreport, and a "hard" news report.

— Ask students to attend and report on a news event (e.g.; city, town, band, or municipal council meeting). Have them compare their report and coverage with that of classmates. What did each student emphasize? What was ignored or left out? Why? What does this reveal about the assumptions of the reporter? Have students compare their reports with reports of the same event in the local paper. What did the newspaper report emphasize or leave out? What does this suggest about the objectivity of the press? Students could also invite the newspaper reporter to class to discuss the decisions he or she made, and the influence an editor has on such reports.

— Have students analyze several sports stories in a provincial or local newspaper. What is reported? Ask them to consider the following statement: "It is no longer sufficient to write sports stories by numbers or by clichés." Do they agree?

During the first part of this century, flowing phrases adorned the sports pages. However, times have changed. High-quality coverage and writing are just as important in the sports story as the news story. Good sports reporting still includes valuable statistical information and the basics of who won, what the score was, and who starred. However, contemporary sports reporting is more balanced and analytic than in the past. Key plays, direct quotes, records, and views about the significance of sports are also a part of the reporting. Have students report on a sports event in their community. Ask them to report key facts, turning points, quotes, statistics, and analysis. They should avoid a chronological game story approach as well as clichés and biased quotations.

— What cause or idea would students like to see reported in a local newspaper? Have them consider a social, political, personal, or school issue. Ask them to interview the person/people behind the story using basic interviewing strategies including the following:

a) Prepare ahead of time. Know something about the person being interviewed. Write down key questions. Ask why things happened and how they happened. Ask for the person's opinion. Avoid asking yes/no questions.

b) Have a notetaking system. Take a pencil, piece of paper, and, if appropriate, tape recorder.

c) Be courteous. Dress appropriately.

d) Conduct yourself in a professional manner and have confidence in yourself.

e) Be on time. Have a clear idea about how you are going to start.

f) Let the subject do the talking and listen carefully.

g) Write down quotations exactly and record exact spellings of names and titles.

h) Ask the person's permission to call back if the need arises.

i) Remember who the audience is and the type of story you are writing (i.e., a news versus feature story).

j) Write the story the way you want to see it in print.

— Have students prepare a press release for one activity that takes place in their school. Encourage them to answer the 5W+H questions early in the release.

— Information and research are important to a journalist. To become familiar with some of the sources a journalist might employ and those that might be useful, have students determine how each of the following resources might help a professional journalist:

a) a style book

b) a dictionary

c) an atlas

d) a thesaurus

e) a language handbook

f) a legal guide

g) other reference sources

h) the Internet.

— The Internet offers two basic features: communication (e.g., e-mail, newsgroups, chat lines, interactive video and audio) and access to information (e.g., libraries, governmental and private agencies and departments, businesses, individuals). Although the Internet can be a source of useful, factual information, it can also be a source of opinion, gossip, exaggerations, hatred, pornography, falsehoods, scams, and hoaxes. Ask students to consider how they might sort out the information and evaluate its credibility. Ask them to choose several potential Internet information sites (e.g., CNN Interactive, Maclean's On-Line, etc.) and evaluate their credibility and usefulness. For each site, they might determine:

a) Why was the information posted? Was it created or modified?

b) Is the information presented fact or opinion or a combination?

c) How can you check or confirm the factual information with at least two other sources?

d) Who is behind the information? Is the creator identified and does the creator have experience or credentials related to the information presented? If an organization is associated with the site (e.g., a government agency, an educational institution, an advocacy group, a non-profit organization, a news agency), do you recognize the name of the organization and is it one that can be trusted?

e) What is the overall "look" of the site? Does it appear professional looking? Sloppy? Splashy? Amateurish? What does the look suggest? Are there cases in which you might distrust a professional-looking site and trust a less professional-looking site? Why or why not?

f) Document each of your sources using an acceptable citation format.

— Have students conduct a search on the Internet for background information for a specific news story. They should frame the essential questions that will guide their search. When they have located their sources, have them review the sources using the criteria outlined above.

— The Internet allows people to construct their own stories. Ask students to consider how they would construct a news story for the Internet. What hypertext links might they include?

— Have students create a "news file" each day on the bulletin board or blackboard. Ask them to identify school, local, national, and international items which they think are newsworthy.

— Have students consider the difference between a hard news story and a soft news story. Who supplies most of the news on the first page?

— Have students take their school's announcement sheet and reduce each announcement to a clear, succinct "news brief" format.

— News stories in Canada do not include reporters' editorial opinions on the issue or event. Good newspaper reports present facts, making their stories as objective as possible. They do not distort facts; nor do they inject their own biases and prejudices into news stories they write. "News English" is marked by the following features:

a) stories begin with key ideas

b) ideas are stated briefly

c) sentences are simple

d) words are clear and unambiguous

e) vivid verbs are used rather than vague or general references to people and places

f) the active voice is employed rather than the passive voice.

g) words are accurate and appropriate.

Newspaper writers avoid sexist or other discriminatory language. They usually use precise and simple words (e.g., "rich" not "opulent"), short sentences, and tight writing to aid the readers. Jargon, clichés, and worn-out figures of speech are avoided. With this in mind, have students edit two of their own and two peers' news stories for these stylistic elements.

Have students examine the journalistic style guidelines outlined in style books such as those published by Associated Press, Canadian Press, and The Globe and Mail. Have students examine one of their own news stories and one news story from a newspaper. How are these stylistic guidelines reflected in each?

The front page of the newspaper usually indicates which news is considered more important by the position of the article and the size of type used for the title or headline. Although there are exceptions, the top right-hand corner often is reserved for the most important news story.

Generally, the size of type in the headline indicates the importance of the news. Have students review with a partner the dailies from the past week. Which news articles seem to be the most important? How can they tell? Which articles or information seem to be the least important? Have them note their conclusions in their journals and compare their comments with those of a peer.

Headlines contain the story's title or summary in larger type above or beside the story. The headlines used to entice the reader are important because they influence the way readers interpret the story and they create a point of view. Have students clip a variety of news stories at random from a national and local paper.

After clipping the stories, ask them to cut off the headlines and number each headline and story to correspond (i.e., #1 story/#1 headline). Have them put all stories in one folder and all headlines in another, then reread each story and write their headline for it. Students might compare their version with their classmates' versions. Finally have them compare their headlines with the original headlines. What conclusions can they draw?

Have students trace a controversial issue in the local press. Have them keep an annotated scrapbook/log on the topic. After several weeks, invite a journalist covering the issue into the classroom to discuss the coverage. How did the journalist determine the issue was newsworthy? How were the facts determined? Were any restrictions placed on the story? By whom and why? How does the journalist ensure balanced and accurate coverage? How does this coverage affect the people involved?

Have students conduct a telephone interview with a classmate. Are telephone interviews more or less accurate than face-to-face interviews? Why? People's lives are affected by the weather. Reporters need a knowledge of weather and the language used to describe it. Ask students to review the weather reports in several newspapers and then to write a weather report for today for their community.

Reporters gather information about disasters (e.g., an airplane crash) and include essential details in their stories (e.g., death count, number of injuries, updates from hospitals, rescue attempts, date, time, background, factors that led to the disaster, latest findings of the investigation, and quotations from witnesses and survivors). What is the difference between factual and sensational reporting? Is there a line to be drawn between human interest and sensationalism when reporting on disasters? What ethical considerations should guide the reporter? Have students imagine a disaster has occurred in their community. Ask them to prepare a report for a provincial or local newspaper.

Some news is the result of press releases. Individuals and groups want to get their stories into newspapers so they prepare and distribute press releases, including details and contact names. Sometimes a press release will be printed with little change and sometimes a reporter will make further inquiries. Have students review several press releases (e.g., government, charitable organization, local club) and then write a news story based on one of these releases.

4

Photojournalism

Good photographs show readers what is happening. Print journalists use photographs to capture attention, break up large areas of print, provide information, provide entertainment, give readers a sense of being there, and show the feelings and reactions of people involved in events.

Learning Objectives

Students will:

— speak to share thoughts, opinions, and feelings

— listen with purpose and concern for ideas

— recognize the importance for journalists of interviewing, researching, and reporting

— identify conventions of feature stories

— understand the major functions of photographs in publications

— recognize the impact of effective photography

— take effective photographs

— understand photo layout, cropping, sizing, and writing cutlines

— recognize how computers and desktop publishing are used in commercial journalism

— experiment with design and layout using a computer and desktop publishing program.

Activities

— Have students view The Best of Life. What was the most powerful image? Why was the image successful? What are the principles of effective photojournalism? How can images add impact to a story? What other features can an image add to a story? Are there some images that should not be shown? Why or why not?

— Have students examine the front pages of several daily newspapers. What photos were used? Why? Were they used effectively? Did they complement the stories? What could be improved?

— Have students take a picture of "their school". "Their school" might mean different things to different people and photos can capture and construct individual perceptions. Have students brainstorm different views and perceptions of their school. They can form groups of five to plan their shots. They can then execute the actual photographing individually. They should plan for each shot and consider whose camera will be used, when and where, the cost, the angle, and the purpose. When the film is developed, they can work in a group to lay the images out in a magazine format (including advertising, cover, and feature stories). As an alternative, they could work alone and write a newspaper story. They should consider: What is their overall message? What are the different means for "shaping the reality" of their school? How will their photograph(s) contribute to the story?

— Have students trace an issue that has been covered over time in the press (newspaper or magazine). Ask them to clip the photos associated with the stories and to mount them in chronological order on a sheet of paper. They should note the name of the publication, the date, and the source, and then evaluate how the photographs, infographics, and art contributed to the coverage. Were they helpful? Were they unethical in any way? Effective? Did the photographs reflect particular points of view?

— Have students shoot a roll of 35 mm film on a particular topic, theme, person, or place. They should pay careful attention to the rule of thirds. Ask them to create a photo essay and to write the accompanying captions and story.

— Have students prepare a photo file for a photo page. They should include a dominant photo, several small photos of varying size, suitable captions, a headline, and a short story. Their work should show good layout/design.

— What topics would make a good full-page photo essay for a school newspaper? Have each student select a topic and take the photos. Students should select the pictures carefully, crop and size them, prepare the layout for the photo page, and write the copy (including cutlines and headlines) that will accompany the photos. Students can exchange work with others and critique each layout and photo.

Magazines

Although magazines follow many of the conventions of the newspaper, there are differences, includingpurpose, appearance, types of stories, intended audience, circulation, and advertising.

Learning Objectives

Students will:

— speak to share thoughts, opinions, and feelings

— listen with purpose and concern for ideas

— analyze and evaluate their own and others' writing

— compare, contrast, and evaluate texts

— recognize the importance for journalists of interviewing, researching, and reporting

— identify conventions of feature stories

— differentiate among the kinds of magazines

— recognize how pervasive information is in contemporary society

— profile a magazine

— understand how magazines serve both readers and advertisers

— evaluate how advertising affects magazine content

— understand organizational patterns of magazine articles

— compare general-interest and special-interest magazines

— compare the design and layout of various magazines

— explain how titles and articles are used to sell magazines

— assess the role magazines play in their lives.

Activities

— Have students bring as many different magazines as possible from the library and from home. Ask them to browse through them and classify each in one of the following categories: sports, news, women's, men's, nature, health and fitness, entertainment, finance, science, hobbies and crafts, farming and ranching, pets, games and puzzles, history, political, travel, cars and motorcycles, humour, literary, romance, science fiction, and mystery. As a class, discuss criteria for judging the quality of a magazine. Students can compare two or more magazines of the same category: How are they alike? How are they different? Do they compete for the same audience or do they appeal to different audiences? Which do students think is the better magazine? Why?

— Have students choose a magazine from those collected and prepare a profile of the magazine based on the following:

a) *Cover*: Notice the title, date, price, picture, and information included on the cover. How does it capture the reader's attention?

b) *Format and Cost*: Notice the size and weight, quality of paper, size/kind/spacing of type, photographs/ illustrations/drawings/cartoons, and use of black-and-white or colour visuals. What impression do these factors make?

c) *Contents*: List the subject of each feature article (e.g., diet). What percentage is fiction? Nonfiction? List the subject matter of each shorter article (e.g., tips, reviews, commentary). Who are the people who contribute to the magazine?

d) *Advertising*: How many pages of ads are included? What percent of the total is this? List the kinds of products advertised and how many ads for each category appear (e.g., six car ads, three travel ads, five personal hygiene product ads). What audience is targeted by the ads? Age? Socio-economic group? Specific interest?

e) *Audience*: To whom is the magazine communicating?

f) *Ownership and Cost*: Who is the publishing company? What other publications does the company produce? With what other enterprises is it associated? What is the cost of one issue? What is the subscription rate? How frequently is the magazine published? Is the magazine worth the cost?

Then, have students prepare a profile of either a popular teen magazine or the person who is the magazine's idealized "target". Does the magazine provide information, entertainment, and advertising that realistically matches the students' lives? Or does it present an ideal world? Is this a world of which they would like to be part?

— Have students select a broad topic such as fashion, money, or poverty. Ask them to brainstorm possible working titles appropriate to their subject. What magazines would be interested in receiving articles with their working titles? They might write an article for one of these magazines.

— Ask students to consider what type of magazine they read most frequently. Sports? News? Women's? Men's? Nature? Health and Fitness? Entertainment? Finance? Science? Hobbies and Crafts? Farming and Ranching? Pets? Games and Puzzles? History? Political? Travel? Cars and Motorcycles? Humour? Literary? Romance? Science Fiction? Mystery? What differences distinguish these categories from each other? What attracts students to these magazines? What magazines would they not want to read at all? Why?

— Ask students to survey their class. What are the most popular magazines? What are the contents of the top three magazines? Have students categorize the articles found in the magazines (e.g., beauty, politics, medicine, fashion, careers, celebrities). How many stories are found in each category? Have students make a list of the people who are depicted in the photographs. Why is a particular person depicted? Does the person have special skills? Knowledge? Wealth? Beauty? How many of the magazines appeal to men and how many to women? Why? What is the portrayal of males and females in illustrations and stories? At what audience is each magazine aimed? How does each cover suggest this? What is each magazine saying about males and females? About different cultural groups?

— Have students find a magazine article that expresses an author's opinion or takes a stand on an issue (not an editorial, column, or review). Ask them to identify the main ideas in the article and explain how the writer developed these ideas. Did the article serve the writer's purpose? Did the style of the article fit the magazine's profile?

— Have students compare and contrast news coverage on one issue in several magazines (e.g., Time, Maclean's, Newsweek, Life, Alberta Report, U.S. News, and World Report). How do the magazines differ from one another in format, content, and tone? How are they similar? Have students note where the stories are placed, how colour is used, and the use of boxed inserts. They should also examine typeface, photo captions, charts, graphs, and maps. What bias is indicated in the different magazines through word choice and the inclusion or exclusion of certain details? How are the different editorial positions of the magazines indicated by their coverage of the news?

— Have students consider the kind of attention they give to magazine advertisements. Have them analyze ten advertisements in male and female fashion magazines. They might examine the claim and the images of each, including:

a) *Visual Features*: General mood of the ad and how it is created, typeface and its location, colour scheme, white space and where the eye is drawn, location and shape of product.

b) *Language Features*: Name of product, tone of language in the ad, claims and appeals (e.g. needs, fears, desires), puns, and other devices.

c) *Advertisement as a Whole*: Major "hooks" it uses to attract and hold attention, propaganda techniques it employs in its claims and images, intended target of the ad, values or ideology underlying the ad, the overall effectiveness of the ad. Does the ad appeal to reason, emotions, or both? Which ad is the most effective? Why?

— Have students create their own ad. Ask them to review the Canadian Code of Advertising Standards. Does their ad meet the standards?

— Have students review and then plan an electronic magazine for the Internet. Have them consider their purpose, audience, appearance, types of stories, links, and advertising.

5

Computer Communication

By the 1990s, a look backward saw three distinct phases in computing machinery, based on the primary electronic device that classified as::

— First generation: vacuum tubes (ENIAC, UNIVAC)

— Second generation: transistors (IBM 7090)

— Third generation: integrated circuits (IBM 360 series)

Transistors are better than tubes because they are cheaper, more reliable, smaller, faster, and generate less heat. Integrated circuits are built on tiny solid-state chips that combine many transistors in a very small space. Well, all of the computing power of the IBM 7090, which filled a good-sized room when it was introduced in 1966, is now packed into a chip the size of our fingernail. Made such complicated things so small by the way of a photo-engraving process.

The circuits are designed on paper, photographed so that a lens reduces the image—just the way your camera reduces the image of your house to fit on a frame of 35 mm. film—and etched on layers of silicon. As computers got better, they got cheaper, but one more thing had to happen before their use could extend to the everyday life of such nonspecialists as journalists. They had to be made easy to use. That is where Admiral Grace Murray Hopper earned her place in computer history. She became the first person to build an entire career on computer programming. Perhaps her most important contribution, in 1952, was her development of the first assembly language. To appreciate the importance of that development, think about a computer doing all its work in binary arithmetic.

Binary arithmetic represents all numbers with combinations of zeros and ones. To do its work, the computer has to receive its instructions in binary form. This fact of life limited the use of computers to people who had the patience, brain power, and attention span to think in binary. Hopper quickly realized that computers were not going to be useful to large numbers of people so long as that was the case, and so she wrote an assembly language. An assembly language assembles groups of binary machine language statements into the most frequently used operations and lets the user invoke them by working in a simpler language that uses mnemonic codes to make the instructions easy to remember.

The user writes the program in the assembly language and the software converts each assembler statement into the corresponding machine language statements—all "transparently" or out of sight of the user—and the computer does what it is told just as if it had been given the orders in its own machine language. That was such a good idea that it soon led to yet another layer of computer languages called compilers. The assembly languages were machine-specific; the compilers were written so that once you learned one you could use it on different machines. The compilers were designed for specialized applications. FORTRAN (for formula translator) was designed for scientists, and more than thirty years and many technological changes later is still a standard.

COBOL (for common business oriented language) was produced, under the prodding of Admiral Hopper, and is today the world standard for business applications. BASIC (for beginners all-purpose symbolic instruction code) was created at Dartmouth College to provide an easy language for students to begin on. It is now standard for personal computers.

To these three layers—machine language, assembler, and compiler—has been added yet a fourth layer. Higher-level special purpose languages are easy to use and highly specialized. They group compiler programs and let the user invoke them in a way that is almost like talking to the computer in plain English. For statistical applications, the two world leaders are SPSS (Statistical Package for the Social Sciences) and SAS (Statistical Analysis System). If you are going to do extensive analysis of computer databases, sooner or later you will probably want to learn one or both of these two higher-level languages. An example that will show why:

You have a database that lists every honorarium reported by every member of Congress for a given year. The first thing you want to know is the central tendency, so you write a program to give you the mean, the variance, and the standard deviation. A FORTRAN program would require 22 steps. In SAS, once the data have been described to the computer, there are just three lines of code. In SPSS there is only one:

SAS:

```
PROC MEANS;
VAR HONOR;
RUN;
```

SPSS:

```
CONDESCRIPTIVE HONOR
```

For a comparative evaluation of SAS and SPSS, keep reading. But first there is one other kind of software you need to know about. Every computer needs a system for controlling its activity, directing instructions to the proper resources. Starting with the first of the third-generation IBM mainframe computers, the language enabling the user to control the operating system was called JCL for Job Control Language. Now "job control language" has become a generic term to mean the language used to run any operating system. The operating systems also include some utility programs that let you do useful things with data like sorting, copying, protecting, and merging files.

One other kind of software is needed for batch computing. If you are going to send the computer a list of instructions, you need a system for entering and editing those instructions. Throughout the 1960s and part of the 1970s, instructions were entered on punched cards. You typed the instructions at a card-punching machine and edited them by throwing away the cards with mistakes and substituting good ones. Today the instructions are entered directly into computer memory and edited there. Older editing systems still in use are TSO (for time-sharing option) and WYLBUR.

XEDIT is a powerful and more recent IBM editor. If you do mainframe computing, you will have to learn one of the editor systems available for that particular mainframe. Personal computer programs that allow batch processing have their own built-in editors, and you can learn them at the same time you learn the underlying program. You can also use the word-processing program with which you are most familiar to write and edit computer programs.

Computers in Modern Age

The first decision to make when approaching a task that

needs a computer is whether to do the job on a mainframe or on a personal computer. The second is what software to use. Software can generally be classified into two kinds: that which operates interactively, generally by presenting you with choices from a menu and responding to your choices, and that which operates in batch mode, where you present a complete list of instructions and get back a complete job. Some statistical packages offer aspects of both.

The threshold of size and complexity at which you need a mainframe keeps getting pushed back. As recently as the early 1980s, a mainframe would routinely be used to analyze a simple public opinion survey with, say, 50 questions and 1,500 respondents. By the late 1980s, personal computers powerful enough to do that job more conveniently were commonplace in both homes and offices. By 1989, USA Today had begun to work with very powerful personal computers to read and analyze large federal government computer archives in its own special projects office. Mainframes were still needed for the larger and more complex databases, but it seems likely that mainframes could become irrelevant for most journalistic work at some point during the shelf life of this book.

After word processing, the most common personal computer applications are spreadsheets and database programs. The best way to get to know a spreadsheet (examples: Lotus, SuperCalc, PC-Calc) is to use one as your personal check register. As a journalist or potential journalist, you are probably more comfortable with words than numbers and don't get your checkbook to balance very often. A spreadsheet will make it possible and may even encourage you to seek out more complicated applications. For example, when Tom Moore was in the Knight-Ridder Washington Bureau, he created a spreadsheet model for a hypothetical federal tax return. Then when Congress debated changes in the tax law, he could quickly show how each proposal would affect his hypothetical taxpayer.

To understand what a database program (examples: dBase, Paradox, PC-File, Q & A) is good for, imagine a project requiring data stored on index cards. A database program will sort things for you and search for specific things or specific relationships. One thing it is especially good for is maintaining the respondent list for a mail survey, keeping track of who has answered, and directing follow-up messages to those who have not.

A database system is better at information retrieval than it is at systematic analysis of the information, but many reporters have used such systems for fairly sophisticated analysis. Those who design computer software and those who decide what software to use have difficult choices to make. Life is a tradeoff. The easier software is to learn and use, the less flexible it is. The only way to gain flexibility is to work harder at learning it in the first place. It is not the function of this book to teach you computer programming, but to give you a general idea of how things work. To do that, this next section is going to walk you through a simple example using SPSS Studentware, a program that is cheap and reliable and achieves a nice balance between flexibility and ease of use.

To ensure that the example stays simple, we'll use only ten cases. But the data are real enough, and they include both continuous and categorical variables. What we have here is a list of the ten largest newspapers according to the September 1988 Audit Bureau of Circulation figures and four data fields for each: 1988 circulation, 1983 circulation, whether or not it is a national newspaper and whether or not it is located in the northeast. On the last two questions, a 1 is entered if it meets the criterion and a 2 is entered if it does not. Here showing what the complete database looks like:

WLSTJL	1869950	2020132	1	1
USATOD	1338734	676095	1	1
NYDNWS	1281706	1395504	2	1
LATIME	1116334	1038499	2	2
NYTIME	1038829	910538	1	1
WAPOST	769318	718842	1	1
CHITRI	715618	751024	2	2
NEWSDA	680926	525216	2	1
DETNEW	677385	650683	2	2
DETFRP	629065	635114	2	2

Before we do anything with it, let's visualize a couple of concepts. In dealing with any set of data, the first thing you need to know is what the unit of analysis is. In this case, the unit is the individual newspaper. Each line in the data is a unit of analysis. Another word for it is observation, which is the term used in SAS manuals. Yet another is case, a term preferred by the writers of SPSS instructions. Each case or observation in the example above is one line or record, to use a common data-processing term. In a larger data set, you might have more than one record per case.

When data were entered on punched cards, the standard record length was 80 characters, which was the width of the standard Hollerith card. Now your data entry medium is more likely to be a magnetic tape or disk, and there is less restriction on record length and therefore less need to have more than one record per case.

However, 80 characters is still a good length if you are likely to want to look at your data on a computer screen. The typical word processor shows an 80-character screen, and if you have to edit the data, the word processor with which you are most familiar can be the best way to do it. Another practical length is 132 characters, the number that will fit on a wide-carriage printer. If you have trouble picturing the concepts of "record" and "unit of analysis," imagine that your data are entered on three-by-five index cards. Each card is a record. What does each card stand for? Is it a person, as in a public opinion poll? A political contribution? A piece of real estate? Whatever it is, that is your unit of analysis.

Here are some other things worth noticing about the simple data set in the example. The identity of each case comes first, and the newspaper names have been compressed to six-character mnemonics. It would be perfectly okay to list the name in full. However, that might take some extra programming because many analysis programs set limits on the length of non-numeric fields that they can handle. Six or eight characters is usually safe. In this data set, we have four fields. The first is alphanumeric, and the other three are numeric. Computers are better at manipulating numeric data and, where we have a choice, we usually prefer all numbers. An identification field is not used for manipulation, as a rule, and so we don't mind not having numbers there. Another thing to note about this data set is that it is in fixed format.

In other words, each field of data lines up (with right justification) vertically. If we think of the character fields as vertical columns, the identification always occupies columns 1 through 6, circulation size is in 8 through 14, prior circulation is in locations 16 through 22, and so forth. Some analysis systems, including both SAS and SPSS, are so forgiving that they don't require this much attention to "a place for everything and everything in its place." They can be made to recognize variables just by the order in which they appear, provided they are delimited.

The data in example are delimited by spaces, meaning there is a space to tell the computer where one field stops and another begins. In some situations, it is better to use commas or other characters as delimiters. In the old punched-card days, delimiters were not used as much because of the limited space. With delimiters, your data are easier for humans to read, even if the computer doesn't care. Now think for a moment about what we might want to do with this data set. One obvious thing is to calculate a mean and a standard deviation for each circulation year. That way, we can see if the ten largest papers as a whole have been declining or growing in circulation.

```
 DATA LIST FILE='PAPER.DOC'/ID 1-6 (A) CIRC88 8-14
CIRC83 16-22 NAT 24 NOREAST 26.
 COMPUTE GROWTH = (CIRC88-CIRC83)/CIRC83.
 FREQUENCIES                    VARIABLES=ALL/
STATISTICS=DEFAULT
MEDIAN.
LIST VARIABLES=ID GROWTH.
```

Four simple commands:

— *Data list* : This is a format statement. It tells SPSS to look in its own directory for the file named "PAPER.DOC." How did the file get there? It then tells SPSS that the first variable is named ID, that it is found in positions 1 through 6 and that it is alphanumeric rather than numeric (the default). Then each of the other variables is named and its location given.

— *Compute*: This is a powerful SPSS command for making new variables out of old ones. This particular statement says that, for each case, subtract the old circulation from the new and divide the result by the old. That, of course, yields the percent change from 1983 to 1988. The command further tells SPSS to assign the resulting value to a new variable named GROWTH.

— *Frequencies:* This simple command tells SPSS to report the frequency of each occurrence of each value for each variable in three ways; absolute terms, simple percent, and cumulative percent. The STATISTICS option further orders the mean, median, standard deviation, and range for each variable.

— *List* is asking for a simple report showing the five-year circulation shift for each newspaper.

The total output from these four simple commands is three pages long. The important part can be summarized quite succinctly. The mean circulation for these ten papers rose from 932,165 to 1,022,786 over the five-year period. To see which grew and which shrank, here is a direct quote from the SPSS output:

ID	GROWTH
WLSTJL	-.07
USATOD	.98
NYDNWS	-.08
LATIME	.07
NYTIME	.14
WAPOST	.07
CHITRI	-.05
NEWSDA	.30
DETNEW	.04
DETFRP	-.01

The papers appear in the order of their size in 1988. You would rather see the list sorted by growth? No problem. SPSS will sort it, or you can copy the output to your word processor and sort it there. Either way, the result will look like this:

ID	GROWTH
USATOD	.98
NEWSDA	.30
NYTIME	.14
LATIME	.07
WAPOST	.07
DETNEW	.04
DETFRP	-.01
CHITRI	-.05
WLSTJL	-.07
NYDNWS	-.08

Which papers have experienced the most growth, national or local, northeast or elsewhere? There are at least two convenient ways to test this. One is to get the mean growth for each category. Another is to reduce the GROWTH variable itself to categorical status and run a crosstab. To do that, we'll take the top five on the list and call them the high-growth papers, and the remainder the low or no-growth papers. Here is the SPSS code for comparing the means:

Means Growth by NAT Noreast:

That produces output that tells you that the mean growth for each of the subgroups was:

National papers	.2792
Non-national papers	.0457
Northeast	.2220
Non-northeast	.0148

Of course, these means are severely impacted by USA Today, a national paper published in the northeast with a 98 percent growth rate across these five years. To minimize its influence, we can cut back to the categorical level of measurement and just classify all the papers as high growth or low growth. The SPSS code to do that (and introduce some labels on the output to make the tables easy to read) is as follows:

```
COMPUTE GROWCAT=1.

IF (GROWTH GT .04) GROWCAT=2.

VALUE LABELS GROWCAT 1 'LOW' 2 'HIGH'.

VALUE LABELS NAT NOREAST 1 'YES' 2 'NO'.

CROSSTABS TABLES = GROWCAT BY NAT
NOREAST/OPTIONS 4.
```

The first line computes a new variable called GROWCAT (for growth category) and sets it to an initial value of 1 for each case. The second line tells the computer to evaluate each case and if its value for GROWTH is greater than .04, to change GROWCAT from a 1 to a 2. That leaves each case classified as a 1 or a 2 depending on whether its value was high or low. The next line gives labels to those values so you won't forget them. Another VALUE LABELS command labels the national and northeast variables for the same reason.

National papers and those in the northeast still have an edge. Seventy-five percent of the national papers but only half of the local ones were in the high circulation gain group. Two-thirds of the northeast papers and only half of the others enjoyed high growth. Of course, statistical tests, such as chi-square, are easily added.

Comparison of SPSS and SAS

Both systems are constantly being improved and

expanded, and so any comparison between them risks becoming quickly outdated. However, as late as 1990, there were fundamental differences in approach traceable to the respective corporate cultures of SAS and SPSS, which did not seem likely to change over time.

SAS was more of a programmer's system, SPSS was better suited to the nonprogrammer. In the tradeoff between flexibility and ease of use, SAS leaned a little more toward flexibility. If you were going to analyze data often, that is, more than two or three times a year, it could be worth the trouble to master SAS. With SPSS you did not have to think like a programmer. Some steps that SAS kept visible in order to force you to understand what was happening in the computer were made transparent by SPSS. This was particularly true where crosstabs were concerned. Labeling and setting up tables was much easier in SPSS.

SAS justly gained fame for its file management capabilities. If you had large and complicated bodies of data to work with on a mainframe, SAS was great at letting you reshape them and get them into workable form. Both SAS and SPSS were, by the late 1980s, capable of reading complicated formats, some of which will be discussed shortly. The weakest point for SAS was its manuals. Those produced in the 1980s were written by programmers for programmers, and, until you learned to think like a computer programmer, they were hard to read. The SAS folks cranked them out so fast that they sometimes did not get them organized well. An early introduction to SAS-PC, for example, told you clearly, with four-color illustrations, how to save a program file, but it never mentioned how to retrieve it once it was saved. SPSS manuals were more readable.

Marija Norusis has produced a series of books for SPSS which integrate the explanation of computer technique and statistical method, which is the logical way to learn this stuff. In their PC versions, SAS and SPSS designed very different editors, the systems that let you prepare your batch instructions. The SPSS editor was combined with a menu system. This is good news for personal computer users who are likely to be accustomed to menus, but SPSS, like SAS, is meant for batch mode. Most newcomers to SPSS used the menus like training wheels and bypassed them for direct entry as soon as possible. The SAS editor, called "Display Manager," was more logical and easier to learn than the SPSS version. It gave you three screens: one for your batch program, one for the output, and one for the log that recorded the good or bad things that happened to your program, including the error messages. One key let you toggle between the three screens, and another key let you zoom any of them up to a full screen so you could concentrate on its contents.

Both SAS and SPSS had only minor differences in their mainframe and PC languages. Both SAS and SPSS had systems for exporting their system files--files with the format and label instructions already carried out—between mainframes and PCs. And at the mainframe level, SPSS and SAS could read each other's system files, a clever move designed to encourage users of one to switch to the other without worrying about losing the value of their existing data libraries. The SAS v. SPSS story is a fine example of the power of competition in a free market system. Each keeps trying to outdo the other. Many users, afraid of being left behind in some new development, maintain a bilingual capability.

Databases

A database that follows the model of the ten largest newspapers used earlier in this chapter is straightforward and easy to work with no matter how large it gets. If we had 2,000 newspapers and 2,000 variables (4 million pieces of information), the logic and the programming would be exactly the same as we used with ten papers and five variables. Such a database is called rectangular. Every case has the same number of records and the same number of variables. There are two fairly common types of nonrectangular files:

— Files with different numbers of records per case.

— Files that are hierarchical or nested.

In the first of these two cases, a file can be treated as if it were rectangular with the variables that would have been in the missing records defined as "missing." Both SAS and SPSS provide for automatic treatment of missing values. When calculating percentages, for example, they use the number of nonmissing values as the base.

For example, if you had a file describing the 83 residents of a dormitory, and if 40 were classified as males, 40 as females, and the gender of three was unknown, either system would report 50 percent males and 50 percent females unless you specified missing as a separate category.

But sometimes an unequal number of records does not denote missing values. It may just mean different quantities of whatever is being measured. A hierarchical file is one way of dealing with this situation. Suppose the government created a computer file based on reports filed by manufacturing companies on their disposition of toxic waste. The unit of analysis (or case or observation) would be a single plant. Then there might be one record for each toxic chemical emitted, with each record showing how much of the chemical was discharged in each of several sectors of the environment, e.g., land, water, air, or recycling facility. A plant that dumped a lot of different chemicals would have more records per case than a plant that dumped a few. Both SAS and SPSS are equipped to handle this situation.

Suppose there is one report for each corporate entity that emits toxic waste. The first record in each case would have information about the corporation, it size, location of headquarters, industrial classification, and so on. Call this Record Type 1. For each of these corporate records, there is a set of plant records, one for each plant. This would be Record Type 2, and it would contain information about the plant, including geographic location, size, product line, etc.

For each plant record, there would be yet another set of records (Type 3), one for each toxic chemical discharged. Each of these records would give the generic name for the chemical, any trade names, the amount, an indication of its form (gas, liquid, or solid).

Finally, for each chemical record, envision one more set (Type 4), one for each method of disposal used for that particular chemical, i.e., ground, water, air, recycling. Each of these records could give details on the time, place, and manner of each emission.

If all of that sounds complicated, it is because it is. However, there is some good news here. The good news is that a flexible analysis package like SAS or SPSS can deal with this kind of file, and, even better, it can let you choose the unit of analysis. Hierarchical files are created by people who don't have the slightest idea what the analyst will eventually be interested in, and so the files are designed to leave all possibilities open. The advantage is that you can set your unit of analysis at any level in the hierarchy. Suppose, for example, you want the individual plant to be the unit of analysis.

The computer can spread the corporate data across all of the plant cases so that you can use the corporate variables in comparing the characteristics of different plants. Or if you want the individual chemical emission to be the unit of analysis, you can tell the computer to spread the corporate and plant data to cover each emission. You do that by creating a rectangular file first. After that, the rest of the analysis is straightforward.

COMPUTERS COMMUNICATION

The first law of computers seemed to be "Everything is incompatible.", twenty years ago. Today, compatibility is usually close at hand. While computers use binary formats to hold and process information, there are a number of possible ways to do it. The smallest unit of information is the binary "bit," meaning one piece of on-off, yes-no, open-closed information. By stringing several bits together, one can encode more complicated pieces of information, and the standard convention is to string them together in groups of eight. Each group of eight is called a "byte."

When a computer manufacturer tells you that a machine has 512K of random access memory, it means 512 kilobytes or 512,000 bytes. A byte is also the equivalent of a letter, number, or special character on the keyboard. For example in the Extended Binary-Coded Decimal Interchange Code (EBCDIC), standard on IBM mainframes, the eight-bit expression 11010111 stands for the letter "P." Another coding system, the American Standard Code for Information Exchange (ASCII), is used on most personal computers. Right there you can sense some problems if you try to move data from one kind of computer to another, but they have been mostly anticipated by the designers of the communication equipment.

If you move data between a mainframe and a personal computer, the communication software takes care of the ASCII-EBCDIC conversion, and you seldom have to be aware of the difference. The telephone is convenient for data sets that are not too large. Their speeds are measured in baud rates, after the Baudot code. Low-priced modems in 1989 operated at 1,200 baud, which is about

120 characters per second or 1,200 words per minute--more than most people's comfortable reading speed. More expensive equipment was capable of 9,600 baud. Even so, for very large data sets to be moved across phone lines takes a considerable amount of time, and there were still situations where it was more convenient to move data from one place to another by physically carrying it in a magnetic or optical medium.

A development that helped some news organizations was the availability of a desktop tape drive that could transfer the contents of a tape written on a mainframe to a personal computer. USA Today installed one in 1989. A local area network, or LAN, provides a means of moving data among computers over short distances. Dealing with large government databases usually means having to work with tapes unless you can talk the governmental unit into copying the material onto personal computer disks. Tapes are more complicated than disks only because there are more ways to store data on them. When you tackle a tape data set for the first time, you will probably be working with a mainframe, and you can expect help from the computer professionals at the mainframe installation.

If you have a good description of the tape, that person can put together the job control language (JCL) to read it and boot SAS or SPSS. You don't have to learn to do everything yourself, at least not all at once. But you will find it easier to communicate with the pros if you know the following facts about how tape data sets are constructed.

Tape Facts

The data are stored on tracks which run the length of the tape. Nine-track is the standard IBM format, but some systems still use seven tracks. Before a tape can be written on for the first time, it has to be initialized, which usually means giving it an internal, machine-readable label and specifying a density range. The most common density levels are 1,600 and 6,250 bytes per inch (BPI). The key variables for the data layout are logical record length (LRECL in job control language) and block size (BLKSIZE).

Because a tape drive reads the data sequentially, spooling through the tape from the beginning to find what it is told to look for, it pays to pack the records in cheek-to-cheek to reduce the distance the tape has to travel, and so the records are "blocked." If a tape has an LRECL of 80 and BLKSIZE of 80, each logical record is its own block, and the data are said to be in "card image," because the physical records are analogous to a deck of old-fashioned Hollerith cards. You will also need to specify the record format (RECFM), which is usually FB for fixed format (i.e., each record is the same length), and the records are arranged in blocks. These characteristics are all specified on a JCL statement that describes the Data Control Block (DCB).

Many different data sets can be kept on one tape. You might store a dozen public opinion polls on one tape, for example. To keep track of them, the computer leaves an end-of-file (EOF) marker at the end of each data set that it writes. To get back to that same data set, you just specify its sequence number in the JCL statement. Two EOF marks together constitute the end-of-tape signal. It helps to keep the tape from running off the reel and flopping foolishly around.

When you use an IBM standard label tape, you can often ignore most of the DCB business because it is contained in the tape's own internal label and your computer software will read it and adjust things for you. Here is an example of a JCL data definition statement for reading a standard label tape:

```
//INPUT DD DSN=TUCIRSS.ROPER.GSS7288.SPSSX,
LABEL=(1,SL), VOL=SER=UDL393,DISP=OLD,
UNIT=TAPE
```

The two slashes tell the computer that it is reading job control language. INPUT DD means that it is about to receive the data definition for an incoming file. The four strings of characters separated by periods are the tape's internal, machine-read label. LABEL=(1,SL) means that this is an IBM standard label tape, and the machine is to read the first file on the tape. UDL393 is the external label on the tape. A human being has to locate it by that label, pick it off a shelf, and mount it on a tape drive.

If this were not a standard label tape, or if you were uncertain, you could bypass the label processing and spell out the DCB characteristics in that same statement. Sometimes very large data sets, especially those prepared by or for the federal government, use some special coding systems designed to save space. They use hexadecimal or zoned decimal or packed decimal notation. Not to worry. Both SAS and SPSS have provisions to allow you to warn the computer in the input statement to watch out for that stuff.

As long as you tell the computer what to expect, there is no problem, and the output will show the conventional numbers you want. Data formats are more standardized in a personal computer, and you seldom have to worry about the details of how information is laid out on a disk. But you will want to keep an operating system manual handy, for its utilities if for nothing else. The companies that write operating system software tend to issue manuals that are compulsive in their completeness. This makes them hard to read. Browse in the computer department of a good bookstore until you find a manual by an independent author that is pitched at your level. Microsoft DOS (Disk Operating System) was the standard for IBM and compatible computers throughout the 1980s. A newer system, OS/2, was designed to allow more efficient use of resources by permitting a personal computer to work on more than one task at once.

Nerd Factor

Computers are so fascinating in and of themselves that it is easy to get so absorbed in the minutia of their operation that you forget what you started to use the computer for in the first place. The seductive thing about the computer is that it presents many interesting puzzles for which there is always an answer. And if you work with it long enough and hard enough, it will always reward you.

Most of life is not that way. Rewards are uncertain; you never have complete control. And so it becomes tempting to concentrate on the area where you do have control, the computer and its contents, to the exclusion of everything else. Neither academics nor journalists can afford to become that narrow. The computer needs to be kept in its place: as a tool to help you toward a goal, not as the goal itself.

You can't learn everything there is to know about computers, but you can learn what you need to know to get the story. You will find that concepts and procedures that you do not use more than once are quickly forgotten, and that you will build two kinds of knowledge: things you need to know and do yourself, and things for which you can find ready help when you need it. Be a journalist first, and don't use the computer to shut out the world.

6

Nature and Functions of News

News is the reporting of current events usually by local, regional or mass media in the form of newspapers, television and radio programs, or sites on the World Wide Web. News reporting is a type of journalism, typically written or broadcast in news style. Most news is investigated and presented by journalists (or reporters) and often distributed via news agencies. If the content of news is significant enough, it eventually becomes history. To be considered news, an event usually must have broad interest due to one or more news values:

— Impact (how many people were, are or will be affected?)

— Timeliness (did the event occur very recently?)

— Revelation (is there significant new information, previously unknown?)

— Proximity (was the event nearby geographically?)

— Entertainment (does it make for a fun story?)

— Oddity (was the event highly unusual?)

— Celebrity (was anyone famous involved?)

News coverage often includes the "five W's and the H" — who, what, where, when, why, and how. In democracies, news organizations are often expected to aim for objectivity: reporters cover both sides in a controversy and try to eliminate bias. This is not true of all organizations in all cultures. For instance, British television news is required to be objective, but the newspapers are expected to have a point of view; however, limits are set by the government agency Ofcom, the Office of Ccmmunications. The UK has stricter libel laws than the US for the press.

In contrast, both newspapers and broadcast news programs in the U.S. are generally expected to remain neutral and avoid bias except for clearly indicated editorial articles or segments. Many single-party states have operated state-run news organizations, which may present the government's views. Even in those situations where objectivity is expected, it is difficult to achieve, and individual journalists may fall foul of their own personal bias, or succumb to commercial or political pressures. Individuals and organizations who are the subject of news reports may use news management techniques to ensure that they make a favourable impression.

The word "news" comes from a special use of the plural of the word "new", and not as the common backronym claims, from the four cardinal directions (North, East, West, and South). Old spellings of the word varied widely-newesse, newis, nevis, neus, newys, niewes, newis, nues, etc-which casts doubt on this popular etymological theory. A news junkie is a term for a person who likes to keep up to date with the latest news, perhaps

A weblog (usually shortened to blog, but occasionally spelled web log) is a web-based publication consisting primarily of periodic articles (normally in reverse chronological order). Although most early weblogs were manually updated, tools to automate the maintenance of such sites made them accessible to a much larger population, and the use of some sort of browser-based software is now a typical aspect of "blogging".

Blogs range in scope from individual diaries to arms of political campaigns, media programs, and corporations. They range in scale from the writings of one occasional author, to the collaboration of a large community of writers. Many weblogs enable visitors to leave public comments, which can lead to a community of readers centered around the blog; others are non-interactive. The totality of weblogs or blog-related websites is often called the blogosphere. When a large amount of activity, information and opinion erupts around a particular subject or controversy in the blogosphere, it is sometimes called a blogstorm or blog swarm.

The format of weblogs varies, from simple bullet lists of hyperlinks, to article summaries or complete articles with user-provided comments and ratings. Individual weblog entries are almost always date and time-stamped, with the newest post at the top of the page, and reader comments often appearing below it. Because incoming links to specific entries are important to many weblogs, most have a way of archiving older entries and generating a static address for them; this static link is referred to as a permalink. The latest headlines, with hyperlinks and summaries, are frequently offered in weblogs in the RSS or Atom XML format, to be read with a feed reader.

The tools for editing, organizing, and publishing weblogs are variously referred to as "content management systems", "publishing platforms", "weblog software", and simply "blogware".

Electronic communities existed before internetworking. For example the AP wire was, in effect, similar to a large chat room where there were "wire fights" and electronic conversations. Another pre-digital electronic community Amateur (or "ham") radio allowed individuals who set up their own broadcast equipment to communicate with others directly. Ham radio also had logs called "glogs" that were personal diaries made using wearable computers in the early 1980s.

Before blogging became popular, digital communities took many forms, including Usenet, email lists and bulletin boards. In the 1990s Internet forum software, such as WebX, created running conversations with threads. Many of the terms from weblogging were created in these earlier media.

Blogging combined the personal web page with tools to make linking to other pages easier, specifically blogrolls and TrackBacks, as well as comments and afterthoughts. This way, instead of a few people being in control of threads on a forum, or anyone able to start threads on a list, there was a moderating effect that was the personality of the weblog's owner. Justin Hall, who began eleven years of personal blogging in 1994 while a student at Swarthmore College, is generally recognized as one of the earliest bloggers.

The term "weblog" was coined by Jorn Barger in December 1997. The shorter version, "blog", was coined by Peter Merholz, who, in April or May of 1999, broke the word weblog into the phrase "we blog" in the sidebar of his weblog. This was interpreted as a short form of the noun and also as a verb to blog, meaning "to edit one's weblog or a post to one's weblog". One of the pioneers of the tools that make blogging more than merely websites that scroll is Dave Winer. One of his most important contributions was the creation of servers which weblogs would ping to show that they had been updated. Blog reading utilities, such as Blogrolling, use the aggregated update data to show a user when their favorite blogs have new posts.

After the September 11, 2001 attacks, many blogs which supported the U.S. "War On Terrorism" quickly gained readership among a public searching for information to understand that event; many new blogs in the same genre sprang up in this environment. By 2002, many of these were supporting the policy of an invasion of Iraq to remove Saddam Hussein from power and eliminate supposed stockpiles of WMDs. These "war bloggers" came primarily, though not exclusively, from the right side of the political spectrum, and included Instapundit. The term was later broadened to include all bloggers whose focus was the war in Iraq, which spread representation across the political spectrum. By the spring of 2003, Forbes Magazine used "war blogger" in this larger sense when listing the "best warblogs".

The first blog-driven controversy was probably the fall of U.S. Senate Majority Leader Trent Lott, who had remarked, at a party honoring U.S. Senator Strom Thurmond, that Thurmond's leadership abilities may have made him a good President. Since Thurmond had spent much of his early political career sympathetic to white supremacists, Lott's statements were conveyed in the media to be racist. In the aftermath, bloggers such as Josh Marshall strove to demonstrate that his remarks were not an isolated misstatement, by finding evidence including quotes from other previous speeches of Lott's which were taken to be racist. Their efforts kept the story "alive" in the press until a critical mass of disapproval forced Lott to resign his position as Senate Majority Leader.

By this point blogging was enough of a phenomenon that how-to manuals had begun to appear, primarily focusing on using the tools, or creating content. But the importance of a blog as a way of building an electronic community had also been written on, as had the potential for blogs as a means of publicizing other projects. Established schools of journalism began researching the blogging phenomenon, and noting the differences between current practice of journalism and blogging.

Since 2003, weblogs have gained increasing notice and coverage for their role in breaking, shaping, or spinning news stories. One of the most significant events was the sudden emergence of an interest in the Iraq war, which saw both left-wing and right-wing bloggers taking measured and passionate points of view that did not reflect the traditional left-right divide. The blogs which gathered news on Iraq, both left and right, exploded in popularity, and Forbes magazine covered the phenomenon. The use of blogs by established politicians and political candidates-particularly Howard Dean and Wesley Clark-to express opinions on the war and other issues of the day, cemented their role as a news source.

The Iraq war was the first "blog war" in another way: bloggers in Baghdad gained wider readership, and one (Salam Pax) published a book of his blog. Blogs also arose amongst soldiers serving in the Iraq war. Such "milblogs" have given readers a new perspective on the realities of war. Reading the thoughts of people who were "on the spot" provided a supplement and perhaps a differing viewpoint to official news sources. Blogs were often used to draw attention to obscure news sources, for example posting links to the traffic cameras in Madrid as a huge anti-terrorism demonstration filled the streets in the wake of the M11 attacks. By the end of 2003 top rated blogs Instapundit, Daily Kos, and Atrios were receiving over 75,000 unique visitors per day.

In 2004, the role of blogs became increasingly mainstream, as political consultants, news services and candidates began using them as tools for outreach and opinion formation. Even politicians not actively involved in a campaign such as Tom Watson, a UK Labour Party MP, began to use blogging as a means for creating a bond with constituents and creating a channel for their ideas and opinions. Minnesota Public Radio broadcast a program by Christopher Lydon and Matt Stoller called "The

Blogging of the President", which covered the transformation in politics that blogging seemed to presage.

The Columbia Journalism Review began regular coverage of blogs and blogging. Anthologies of blog pieces began to reach print, and blogging personalities began appearing on radio and television. In the summer of that year both the Democratic and Republican National Conventions credentialed bloggers, and blogs became a standard part of the publicity arsenal, with mainstream programs, such as Chris Matthews' Hardball, forming their own blogs. Merriam-Webster's Dictionary declared "blog" as the word of the year in 2004.

Blogs were some of the driving forces behind the "Rathergate" scandal involving Dan Rather of CBS and some memos used on the show 60 Minutes II. Within 72 hours a coordinated group of bloggers had built a case that they were likely forgeries. The evidence presented eventually created such concern over the issue that CBS was forced to address the situation and make an apology for their inadequate reporting techniques. This is viewed by many bloggers as the advent of blogs' acceptance by the mass media as a source of news. It also showed how blogs could keep the pressure on an established news source, forcing defenses and then a retraction of the original story.

Blogging is also used now to break consumer complaints and vulnerabilities of products, in the way that Usenet and email lists once were. One such example is accusations about vulnerability of Kryptonite 2000 locks. Bloggers have also moved over to other media. Duncan Black, Glenn Reynolds, Markos Moulitsas Zúniga, Ana Marie Cox, and others have appeared on radio and/or television. Hugh Hewitt is an example of a media personality who has moved in the other direction, adding to his reach in "old media" by being an influential blogger.

Blogging however, was as much about technology as politics, and the proliferation of tools to run blogs and the communities around them connected blogging with the Open Source movement. Writers such as Larry Lessig and David Weinberger used their blogs to promote not just blogging, but more generally different social models. One of the running discussions within journalism and blogging is what "blogging" means for the way news "happens" and is covered. This leads to questions over intellectual property and the role of the mass media in society.

Many bloggers differentiate themselves from the mainstream media, while others are members of that media working through a different channel. Many bloggers have large agendas, and see blogging as part of Open Source Politics, or the ability of people to participate more directly in politics, helping to frame the debate. Whereas institutions see blogging as a means of "getting around the filter" and pushing message directly to the public.

The free speech imperative of the blog world has also had a deep social impact. For example, a number of companies have clashed with bloggers, firing a few of them. Blogs have also been seen as repositories for information about the state of mind of certain people: in some cases, they could provide insight in the minds of people who committed suicide, people who committed crimes, or people who were victims of a crime.

Since their introduction, a number of software packages have appeared to allow people to create their own weblog. Blog hosting sites and Web services to provide editing via the Web have proliferated. Many more advanced bloggers prefer to generate their blogs by using server-side web applications such as Nucleus CMS, Movable Type, bBlog, WordPress, b2evolution, boastMachine, Antville and Serendipity to publish on their own website or a third party site, or to host a group of blogs for a company or school. Such programs provide greater flexibility and power, but require more knowledge. If they provide a Web interface for editing, server-based systems make it easy for travelers to create and edit text; many travelers like to produce their travelblogs from Internet cafes while they travel around the globe.

In addition, some people program their own blogs from scratch by using PHP, CGI, ASP, Perl, or other server side software. While these are much more difficult to create, they add a maximum potential for creativity. Two features which are common to blogging are "blogrolls" and "commenting" or "feedback." A blogroll is a list of other blogs that are linked separately from any article. This is one means by which a blogger creates a context for his blog, by listing other blogs that are similar to his/her own, or blogs the blogger thinks may be of relevance to users. It is also used as measure of the number of citations a blog has, and is used to rank "blog authority" in a manner similar to the way that Google uses hard coded HTML linking to create "page rank." Still another use of the "blogroll" is reciprocal linking: bloggers agree to link to each other, or link to another blog in hopes of getting a link in return.

Another central, and sometimes controversial, aspect of blogging is the use of a feedback comment systems. A comment system allows users to post their own comments on an article or "thread." Some blogs do not have comments, or have a closed commenting system which requires approval from those running the blog. For other bloggers, including several very prominent ones, comments are the crucial feature which distinguishes a "true" blog from other kinds of blogs. Commenting can either be built into the software, or added by using a service such as HaloScan. If a blog has regular commenters, this is referred to as the blog's community.

Tools such as Ecto and w.bloggar allow users to maintain their Web hosted blog without the need to be online while composing or editing posts. Enhancements to weblog technology continue to be developed, such as the TrackBack feature introduced by Movable Type in 2002 and subsequently adopted by other software companies (e.g., Userland) to enable automatic notification between websites of related content-such as a post on a particular topic or one which responds to a post on another blog. bBlog has gone as far as implementing threaded trackbacks on comments, and comments on trackbacks.

Blogs with features such as TrackBack are credited with complicating search engine page ranking techniques. Integrating these into search engines has proven to be a challenge, and has been used to deliberately "push" page rankings. However, as one Google executive remarked, it is the search engine's job to find the ways that a website represents a "vote" for another website. Web hosting companies and online publications also provide blog creation tools, such as Salon, Tripod, Bravenet and America Online, which calls its subscriber blogs "journals."

Types of Weblogs

Personal

Often, the word blog is used to describe an online diary or journal, such as LiveJournal. The weblog format of an online diary makes it possible for users without much experience to create, format, and post entries with ease. People write their day-to-day experiences, complaints, poems, prose, illicit thoughts and more, often allowing others to contribute, fulfilling to a certain extent Tim Berners-Lee's original view of the World Wide Web as a collaborative medium.

In 2001, mainstream awareness of online diaries began to increase dramatically. Online diaries are integrated into the daily lives of many teenagers and college students, with communications between friends playing out over their blogs. Even fights may be posted in the diaries, with not-so-veiled insults of each other easily readable by all their friends, enemies, and complete strangers.

Thoughtful

Where a personal weblog is primarily concerned with daily life and events, and many topical weblogs focus on some technical topic, weblogs in the "thoughtful" category present an individual's (or a small group's) thoughts on whatever subject comes to hand; not necessarily the latest computer technology or the latest political scandal, but typically less contentious and more philosophical subjects. Thoughtful weblogs of course blur into personal weblogs on one side and topical or political ones on the other, but are distinct enough to constitute a category of their own.

FriendBlog

A FriendBlog is a distributed networked journal on the web, composed of short, frequently updated posts written by friends connected through their similar interests. The author allows his FriendBlog to connect to other FriendBlogs, belonging to friends and acquaintances. This creates a "chain" of blogs.

Topical blogs

Topical blogs focus on a specific niche, often a technical one. An example is Google Blog, covering nothing but Google news. Another example is a soldier blog. Many blogs now allow categories, which means a general blog can be reshuffled to become a topical blog at the user's need.

Many weblogs provide a news digest on a certain topic, e.g., Internet in China, Baseball, Norwegian News in English or Music with short abstracts/summaries and links to interesting articles in the press.

Political blog

Another common kind of blog is a political blog. Often an individual will link to articles from news web sites and post their own comments as well. Many of these blogs comment on whatever interests the author. Some of them are more specialized. One subspecies is the watch blog, a blog which sets out to criticize what the author considers systematic errors or bias in an online newspaper or news site-or perhaps even by a more popular blogger.

Political blogs attracted attention because of their use by two political candidates in 2003: Howard Dean and Wesley Clark. Both gained political buzz on the Internet, and particularly among bloggers, before they were taken seriously by the establishment media as candidates. Joe Trippi, Dean's campaign manager, made the Internet a particular focus of the campaign. Both candidates stumbled in the end, but were, at one time or another, thought of as front runners for the Democratic Nomination.

In 2004, the Democrats took political blogging a major step forward by creating Blog Swarm to coordinate the hypertext links of progressive blogs. This allowed one blog to drive traffic by harnessing the power of a full blog array. Some blogs serve as media watchdogs, reporting on falsehoods or inconsistencies that are presented as facts in the mass media. Many media blogs are focused exclusively on one newspaper or television network.

Given the obvious focus on words, it's not surprising that the Grub Street tradition has continued on the internet with daily commentary emanating from literary blogs (or litblog) such as Bookslut and Maud Newton. Some blogs discuss religious topics. Religious blogs show the public's points of view on various controversies both in religion and in politics, economics, and life in general. Many weblogs are written by more than one person about a specific topic. Collaborative weblogs can be open to everyone or limited to a group of people. MetaFilter is an example of this type of weblog.

Slashdot, whose status as a blog has been debated, nevertheless has a team of editors who approve and post links to technology news stories throughout the day. Although Slashdot does not refer to itself as a weblog, it shares some characteristics with weblogs. A new form of blog represents a fusion of bloggers and traditional media sources, allowing for topics covered in the traditional media to be fleshed out on the web. One prominent early example of this sort of blog is the Dallas Morning News editor's blog.

A partner blog site has a parallel web page or wiki page. Consider the possible similarities between a blog site and a multi-section web document. Blogs are generally thought of as a collection of periodic postings organized by reverse date, each posting its own topic that does not necessarily directly relate to the last. An essay or any large document is also a collection of headings or sub-topics but organized by sequence so that each sub-topic follows from the last to form a coherent whole. An example of this partnership is Blog Study, which has a sidebar link to a parallel web page.

At the blog site readers can use the comments link to discuss each section. The author or authors of both sites having the passwords to both would keep these two parallel, building on the feedback and re-weaving it into the section of the web page essay and re-editing the original blog posting. Revisions to the web page would come after consensus formed in the posting at the blog site. The web page provides a streamlined printout or reading without the distractions of the comment and date data. The comments section of the blog provides a way to track, remember and negotiate each heading section of the document.

The web page also provides more secure control of the developing document than with a wiki, but slows down the evolution of the more comprehensive document. A troika partnership of web, wiki and web page is also viable. This has a wide range of uses for group editing of policy statements, manuals, and grant and curriculum development. There are many educational applications of blogs. Students can use weblogs as records of their learning and teachers can use weblogs as records of what they taught. For example, a teacher can blog a course, recording day-by-day what was taught, including links to Internet resources, and specifying what homework students are required to carry out. This application has many advantages: (1) a student can quickly catch-up if they miss a class; (2) the teacher can use the blog as a course plan; and (3) the blog serves as an accurate summary of the course that prospective students or new teachers can refer to.

There are other educational applications of blogs. Students can blog an educational excursion, recording day-by-day (or hour by hour) where they went, what they saw and what they learned - including photographs, audio or video. The collaborative features of blogs can be used to permit several students to contribute to the blog. Blogs can be used by a wide range of educational organisations. Directory weblogs are useful for web-surfers because they often collect numerous web sites with interesting content in an easy to use and constantly updated format. News-related weblogs can fall into this category or the previous one (political blogs).

With the rise in popularity of blogs in 2004 senior management caught on to the trend and by January 2005 several types of organizations, including universities, had started using blogs to communicate with their stakeholders. Many believe this corporate takeover of a tool that was used primarily by Internet enthusiasts will lead to a decrease in the popularity of the medium. Others believe that the use of blogs by organizations will add new voices and vitality to the medium. At any rate, there is little evidence that the growth rate of the blogosphere has slowed. A prime example of senior management blogging is GM's Fastlane blog, edited, among others, by GM vice chairman Bob Lutz.

Many weblogs provide expert advice, such as Microsoft technical knowledge (GaryDev) or fiction publishing for women. Many small businesses are also using blogs to offer advice and better connect with their clients. These blogs are particularly prevalent in the real estate industry where agents typically have a great deal of flexibility in marketing themselves. Some weblogs specialize in particular forms of presentation, such as images, or videos, or on a particular theme, and acronyms have been developed for some of these, such as moblogs (for "mobile" blog).

One of the types of blog that has undergone rapid expansion since the year 2000 is the MP3 blog, which make audio files available to the user. MP3 blogs are normally targeted at highly specialized musical genres, such as late 60s soul music or early 90s hip-hop or even the latest stuff in electronic dance music genres like grime. However, personal audioblogs are also on the rise.

7

Photography

Photography is the process of making pictures by means of the action of light. It involves recording light patterns, as reflected from objects, onto a sensitive medium through a timed exposure. The process is done through mechanical, chemical or digital devices commonly known as cameras.

Lens and mounting of a large format camera

Most commonly a camera or camera obscura is the image forming device and photographic film or a digital storage card is the recording medium, but other methods are available. For instance, the photocopy or xerography machine forms permanent images but uses the transfer of static electrical charges rather than photographic film, hence the term electrophotography.

The rayographs published by Man Ray in 1922 are images produced by the shadows of objects cast on the photographic paper, without the use of a camera. And one can place objects directly on the glass of a scanner to produce pictures electronically. Photographers control the camera to expose the light recording material (usually film) to light. After processing, this produces an image whose contents are acceptably sharp, bright and composed to achieve the objective of taking the photograph. The controls include:

— Focus

— Aperture of the lens

— Duration of exposure (or shutter speed)

— Focal length of the lens (telephoto, macro, wide angle, or zoom)

— Sensitivity of the film

The controls are usually inter-related, for example brightness is aperture multiplied by shutter speed, and varying the focal length of the lens will allow greater control over the depth of field.

Photography can be classified under imaging technology and has gained the interest of scientists and artists from its inception. Scientists have used its capacity to make accurate recordings, such as Eadweard Muybridge in his study of human and animal locomotion (1887). Artists have been equally interested by this aspect but have also tried to explore other avenues than the photo-mechanical representation of reality, such as the pictorialist movement. Military, police and security forces use photography for surveillance, recognition and data storage.

History of Photography

Projecting images onto surfaces has been done for centuries. The camera obscura and the camera lucida were used by artists to trace scenes as early as the 16th century. These early cameras did not fix an image in time; they only projected what was before an opening in the wall of a darkened room onto a surface. In effect, the entire room was turned into a large pinhole camera. Indeed, the phrase camera obscura literally means "darkened room," and it is after these darkened rooms that all modern cameras have been named. The first photograph is considered to be an image produced in 1826 by the French inventor Nicéphore Niépce on a polished pewter plate covered with a petroleum derivative called bitumen of Judea. It was produced with a camera, and required an eight hour exposure in bright sunshine.

However this process turned out to be a dead end and Niépce began experimenting with silver compounds based on a Johann Heinrich Schultz discovery in 1724 that a silver and chalk mixture darkens when exposed to light. Niépce, in Chalon-sur-Saône, and the artist Jacques Daguerre, in Paris, refined the existing silver process in a joint partnership. In 1833 Niépce died unexpectedly of a stroke, leaving his notes to Daguerre. While he had no scientific background, Daguerre made two pivotal contributions to the process. He discovered that by exposing the silver firstly to iodine vapour, before exposure to light, and then to mercury fumes after the photograph was taken, a latent image could be formed and made visible. By then bathing the plate in a salt bath the image could be fixed.

In 1839 Daguerre announced that he had invented a process using silver on a copper plate called the Daguerreotype. A very similar process is still used today for Polaroids®. The French government bought the patent and immediately made it public domain. Across the English Channel, William Fox Talbot had earlier discovered another means to fix a silver process image but had kept it secret. After reading about Daguerre's invention, Talbot refined his process, so that it might be fast enough to take photographs of people as Daguerre had done, and by 1840 he had invented the calotype process. He coated paper sheets with silver chloride to create an intermediate negative image.

Unlike a daguerreotype, a calotype negative could be used to reproduce positive prints, like most chemical cameras do today. Talbot patented this process, which greatly limited its adoption. He spent the rest of his life in lawsuits defending the patent until he gave up on photography all together. But later this process was refined by George Eastman and is today the basic technology used by chemical film cameras. Hippolyte Bayard also developed a method of photography, but delayed announcing it and so was not recognized as its inventor.

The Daguerreotype proved popular as it responded to the demand for portraiture emerging from the middle classes during the Industrial Revolution. This demand, that could not be met in volume and in cost by oil painting, may well have been the push for the development of photography. But still daguerreotypes, while beautiful, were fragile and difficult to copy. A single photograph taken in a portrait studio could cost $1000 in 2005 dollars. Photographers also encouraged chemists to refine the process of making many copies cheaply, which eventually lead them back to Talbot's process.

The modern photographic process came about from a series of refinements and improvements in the first 20 years. In 1884 George Eastman, of Rochester New York, developed dry gel on paper, or film, to replace the photographic plate, so that a photographer no longer needed to carry boxes of plates and toxic chemicals around. In July of 1888 Eastman's Kodak camera went on the market with the slogan "You press the button, we do the rest". Now anyone could take a photograph and leave the dangerous portions of the process to others. Photography became available for the mass-market in 1901 with the introduction of a children's camera, the Kodak Brownie and a women's camera that came with a free lipstick.

Very little has changed in chemical photography since then, though color film has become the standard, as well as automatic focus and automatic exposure. Digital recording of images is becoming increasingly prevalent, as digital cameras allow instant previews on LCD screens among other benefits, and the definition of top of the range models have become comparable to high quality 35mm film while lower definition models have become affordable. For the enthusiast photographer processing black and white film, little has changed since the introduction of the 35mm film Leica camera in 1925.

In the nineteenth century, photography developed rapidly as a commercial service. In the U.S. in 1890, the number of professional photographers was about the same as the number of accountants, artists, and dentists, respectively, and about ten times greater than the number of authors. End-user supplies of photographic equipment accounted for only about 20% of industry revenue. Several trends characterize the photographic industry from the end of the nineteenth century to the end of the twentieth century. The ratio of revenue from end-user photographic supplies to revenue from professional services rose by an order of magnitude.

The prevalence of personal cameras and the ratio of end-user photographs rose closely in tandem with the prevalence of telephone and the telephone conversation minutes. However, the ratio of photographic industry revenue to telephone industry revenue dropped sharply.

Given the development of new digital technologies for creating and sharing images, and of new communications devices, e.g. camera phones, understanding the economics of image use are becoming increasing important for understanding the evolution of the communications industry as a whole.

Color Photography

Color photography was explored throughout the 1800s. Initial experiments in color could not fix the photograph and prevent the color from fading. The first permanent color photo was taken in 1861 by the physicist James Clerk Maxwell. One of the early methods of taking color photos was to use three cameras. Each camera would have a color filter in front of the lens. This technique provides the photographer with the three basic channels required to recreate a color image in a darkroom or processing plant. The first color film, Autochrome, did not reach the market until 1907 and was based on dyed dots of potato starch. The first modern color film, Kodachrome, was introduced in 1935 based on three colored emulsions.

Most modern color films, except Kodachrome, are based on technology developed for Agfacolor (as 'Agfacolor Neue') in 1936. Instant color film was introduced by Polaroid in 1963. Color photography may form images as a positive transparency, intended for use in a slide projector or as color negatives, intended for use in creating positive color enlargements on specially coated paper. The latter is now the most common form of film (non-digital) color photography, owing to the introduction of automated photoprinting equipment.

Traditional Photography

Traditional photography was a considerable burden for photographers working at remote locations (such as press correspondents) without access to processing facilities. With increased competition from television, there was pressure to deliver their images to newspapers ever faster. Photo-journalists at remote locations would carry a miniature photo lab with them, and some means of transmitting their images down the telephone line. In 1981, Sony unveiled the first consumer camera to use a CCD for imaging, and which required no film —the Sony Mavica. While the Mavica did save images to disk, the images themselves were displayed on television, and therefore the camera could not be considered fully digital.

In 1990, Kodak unveiled the DCS 100, the first commercially available digital camera. Its cost precluded any use other than photojournalism and professional applications, but commercial digital photography was born. Digital photography uses an electronic sensor such as a charge-coupled device to record the image as a piece of electronic data rather than as chemical changes on film. Some other devices, such as cell phones, now include digital photography features. In 10 years, digital cameras have become widespread consumer products. Digital cameras now outsell film cameras, and many include features not found in film cameras such as the ability to shoot video and record audio.

Kodak announced in January 2004 that it would no longer produce reloadable 35-millimeter cameras after the end of that year. This was interpreted as a sign of the end of film photography, however Kodak was at that time a minor actor on the reloadable film cameras market. The price of 35mm and APS compact cameras have dropped, probably due to direct competition from digital and the resulting growth of the offer of second-hand film cameras. However, "wet" photography may endure, as dedicated amateurs and skilled artists often prefer the use of traditional and familiar materials and techniques.

The greater commercial photographic world is traditionally broken down to:

- *Advertising photography*: photographs done to illustrate a service or product. These images are generally done with an Advertising Agency, Design Firm or with an in-house Corporate design team.
- *Editorial photography* : photographs done to illustrate a story or idea within the context of a magazine. These are usually assigned by the magazine.
- *Photo-journalism* : this can be considered a subset of Editorial. Photographs done in this context are accepted as a truthful documentation of a news story.
- *Portrait & Wedding photography* : photographs done and sold directly to the end user of the images.
- *Fine art photography* : photographs created to fulfill a vision, and reproduced to be sold directly to the end user.

The market for photographic services demonstrates the cliché "one picture is worth a thousand words," which has an interesting basis in the history of photography. Magazines and newspapers, companies putting up Web sites, advertising agencies and other groups pay for photography. Many people take photographs for self-fulfillment or for commercial purposes.

Lighting

The color temperature of a black-body radiator is the actual surface temperature. All other lights, since they are but comparisons to a black-body radiator, should be referred to as having a correlated color temperature (CCT). Incandescent lighting can be described by its CCT. The CCTs of incandescent light sources are determined by comparing the light's color appearance to that of a heated black-body radiator. As the black-body is heated, eventually at a certain point the lamp should match the black-body radiator in color.Whatever the black-body radiator temperature is at that moment is the CCT of this particular light bulb. However, the units of measure used are not degrees Fahrenheit, but kelvins. Lighting is rated using the Kelvin temperature scale, named after the 19th-century British physicist Lord Kelvin.

Depending on the time of day, as the sun crosses the sky, it may appear to be red, orange, yellow, white, or blue. The changing colors of the sky as the day passes each have a CCT too. It will always match a color produced by that black-body radiator at some temperature, measured in kelvins. It is important to match the color sensitivity of your film to the color temperature of your light source. Use tungsten film while photographing indoors with incandescent lamps; the yellow light of the tungsten bulbs will appears as pure white in the prints or slides once the film is processed.

The NTSC and PAL TV norms call for a compliant TV screen to display an electrically "black-and-white" signal (minimal color saturation) at a color temperature of 6500K. On many actual sets however, especially older and/or cheaper ones, there is a very noticeable deviation from this requirement of the standard. Most video and digital still cameras can adjust for color temperature by zooming into a white object and setting the white balance (telling the camera "this object is white"); the camera then shows true white as white and adjusts all the other colors accordingly. White-balancing is necessary especially indoors under fluorescent lighting and when moving the camera from one lighting situation to another. The setting called "Auto white balance" is not recommended for optimum quality video or stills.

Video camera operators can also white-balance objects which aren't white, downplaying the color of the object used for white-balancing. For instance, they can bring more warmth into a picture by white-balancing off something light blue, such as faded blue denim; in this way white-balancing can serve in place of a filter or lighting gel when those aren't available. Cinematographers do not "white balance" in the same way as video camera operators: they can use techniques such as filters, choice of film stock, pre-flashing, and after shooting, color grading (both by exposure at the labs, and also digitally, where digital film processes are used). Cinematographers also work closely with set designers and lighting crews to achieve their desired effects.

The CIE developed a newer model for describing and rating light sources, called the color rendering index, which is a mathematical formula describing how well a light source's illumination of eight sample patches compares to the illumination provided by a reference source. The index provides a number up to 100 for ideal light. The spectral power distributions provided by many manufacturers may have been produced using 10 nanometre increments or more on their spectroradiometer. The result is what would seem to be a smoother (fuller spectrum) power distribution than the lamp actually has. 2nm increments are mandatory for taking measurements of fluorescent lights.

Photojournalism

Photojournalism has been a major element of newspaper and magazine reporting since the early twentieth century, although its historic origins have been traced to mid 19th century European battlefield photography by British press reporters in the Crimean War. Its use was greatly spurred by the development of the commercial 35mm Leica camera. The invention of the term "photojournalism" is commonly attributed to Cliff Edom (1907-1991), who taught at the University of Missouri School of Journalism for twenty-nine years. Edom establish the first photojournalism workshop there in 1946. Some attribute the word, instead, to the then Dean of the School of Journalism, Frank L. Mott.

In the "golden age" of photojournalism (1930s-1950s), some magazines (Picture Post (London), Paris Match (Paris), Life (USA), Sports Illustrated (USA)) and newspapers (The Daily Mirror (London), The Daily Graphic (New York)) built their huge readerships and reputations largely on their use of photography, and photographers such as Robert Capa, Alfred Eisenstaedt, Margaret Bourke-White, W. Eugene Smith became well-known names.

World War II brought a tremendous increase in the supply and demand for quality photojournalism. In its latter stages, the war also stimulated the supply of new faster & smaller cameras from Japan to Europe and the USA. In 1947, two years after World War 2 ended, the Magnum Photos photographic agency was founded by four photographers: Robert Capa, Henri Cartier-Bresson, George Rodger, and David Seymour. Magnum differed from other agencies in that it was a co-operative (all members of the agency were also partial owners). Magnum is still a highly respected photo-agency to this day and membership is extremely selective. There is a review process once a year during which portfolios from applicants are viewed by all current members. From there, the few who are invited to join must withstand a several year probationary period before (with a vote every year by full members to see if the probationary members recent photo work is up to par)they can be considered full members. Many probationary members are asked to leave after one or two years.

Some of the most famous contemporary magnum photographers have left the agency for various reasons either to be independents or to begin their own agencies

(Jim Nachtwey is a founding member of the VII photo agency. Sebastião Salgado founded Amazonia Images). Magnum Photos has more or less been experiencing financial troubles for the last 40 years. Since the late 1970s, photojournalism and documentary photography have increasingly been accorded a place in art galleries alongside art photography. Luc Delahaye, Chin-Chi Chiang, both Magnum photographer to name a few among many exhibit in galleries regularly.

The National Press Photographers Association (NPPA) was the first national organization for newspaper photographers; it was founded in 1946 in the USA, and has approximately 10,000 members. Others around the world include:

— British Press Photographers Association, 1984

— Hong Kong Press Photographers Association, 1989

— Northern Ireland Press Photographers Association, 2000

News organisations and journalism training schools run many different awards for photojournalists. Since 1968, Pulitzer Prizes have been awarded for the following categories of photojournalism: 'Feature Photography', 'Spot News Photography' and 'Capture the Moment'.

Photojournalism works within the same ethical approaches to objectivity that are applied by other journalists. What to shoot, how to frame and how to edit are constant considerations. Often, ethical conflicts can be mitigated or enhanced by the actions of a sub-editor or picture editor, who takes control of the images once they have been delivered to the news organisation. The photojournalist often has no say as to how images are ultimately used. The emergence of digital photography offers whole new realms of opportunity for the manipulation, reproduction, and transmission of images.

It has inevitably complicated many of the ethical issues involved.

The U.S. National Press Photographers Association, and other professional organizations, maintain a Code of Ethics to address what are thought to be the proper approaches to these issues. Major ethical considerations are often enscribed - with more or less success - into law. The law on photography often varies greatly from nation to nation. The legal situation is further complicated when one considers that photojournalism made in one country will often be published in many other countries.

Smaller, lighter cameras greatly enhanced the role of the photojournalist. Since the 1960s, motor-drives, electronic flash, auto-focus, better lenses and other camera enhancements have made their jobs easier. New digital cameras means that photojournalists are no longer limited by the length of a roll of film, as 1000s of images can be stored on a single microdrive or flash card. Content remains the most important element of photojournalism, but the ability to extend deadlines and compress the process of gathering and editing that content has changed greatly. As recently as fifteen years ago, it took nearly thirty minutes to scan and transmit a single color photograph from a remote location to the news office for printing. Now, equipped with a digital camera, a mobile phone and a laptop computer, the print photojournalist can send a high quality image in seconds, only minutes after an event occurs. Video phones and portable satellite links increasingly allow for the mobile transmission of images from almost any point on the earth.

There is some concern amongst news-photographers that photojournalism as a profession as it is known today may change to the degree that it is unrecognizable as image capturing technology naturally progresses. There is also concern that less and less print publications are commissioning serious photojournalism on timely issues.

Print permanence refers to the longevity of printed material, especially photographs. Over time, the color, lustre and other qualities of a print will degrade. The rate at which deterioration occurs depends on two main factors: the ink-type and paper-type combination, and the type of environment the print is exposed to. Dye-based inks last long when used with a specific paper type, whereas pigment-based inks last long on most types of paper. Paper types include swellable paper, porous paper, and cotton rag paper. Environmental factors that hasten the deterioration of a print include exposure to ozone, water, and high levels of light.

Physiology

The viewing of motion pictures appears continuous only because of the slow response of the eye, optic nerves, and brain to changes (called persistence of vision). If your persistence was very short you would perceive a movie as a single frame picture, followed by black, followed by the next frame, etc. It is possible to view the black space between frames and the passing of the shutter by the following technique:

Close your eyelids, then periodically rapidly blink open and closed. If done fast enough you will be able to randomly "trap" the image between frames, or during shutter motion. This will not work with television due to the persistence of the phosphors nor with LCD or DLP light projectors due to the continuity of image, although certain color artifacts may appear with some digital projection technologies.

An incandescent lamp or an electric arc light produces illuminating photons. The traditional carbon arc or modern xenon arc light source produces sufficient heat to burn the film should the film remain stationary for more than a fraction of a second. Xenons were introduced in the 1950s and are now the more common source, being easier and safer to maintain for the most part.

A metal blade which cuts off light before it can get to the film - usually this is part of the lamphouse. Some projectors have both a manually controlled and electronically one each; the electronic one is used for changeovers. Dousers protect the film when the lamp is on but the film is not moving, preventing the film from melting from prolonged exposure to the direct heat of the lamp.

A single image of the series of images comprising the movie is positioned and held flat within an aperture called the gate. The gate also provides a slight amount of friction so that the film does not advance or retreat except when driven to advance the film to the next image.

A rotating petal or gated cylindrical shutter interrupts the emitted light during the time the film is advanced to the next frame. Modern shutters are designed with a flicker-rate of two or even sometimes three times the frame rate of the film, so as to reduce the perception of screen flickering.

A lens system with multiple optical elements directs the image of the film to a viewing screen. Different lenses are used for different aspect ratios. Each of these lenses comes with an aperture plate, a piece of metal with a precisely cut rectangular hole in the middle of equivalent aspect ratio. The aperture plate is placed just behind the gate, and masks off any light from hitting the image outside of the area intended to be shown (most modern films have extra image on the frame that is meant to be masked off in the projector).

In most cases this is a reflective surface which may be either aluminized (for high contrast in moderate ambient light) or a white surface with small glass beads (for high brilliance under dark conditions). In a commercial theater, the screen also has hundreds of small, evenly spaced holes in order to allow the passage of air to and from the speakers and subwoofer which often are directly behind it.

Film Transport Elements

The two reel system is also known as a changeover system, after the switching mechanism that operates between the end of one reel and the beginning of the next. In a two reel system the feed reel has a slight drag to maintain tensioning in the film, while the takeup reel is driven with a constant tension by a mechanism that is allowed to slip. The two reel system was almost universally used before the advent of the single reel system for movie theaters in order to be able to show feature-length films. Although one reel long-play systems tend to be more popular with the newer multiplexes, the two reel system is still in significant use to this day. The projector operator operates two projectors, threading one with the next reel while the other projector plays the current reel.

The current reel approaches its end, the projectionist looks for cues, also known as cigarette burns, at the upper right corner of the picture. Usually these are dots or circles, although they can also be slashes. The first cue appears twelve feet (3.7 m) or eight seconds at 24 frame/s before the end of the reel, and signals the projectionist to start the motor of the projector containing the next reel. After another ten and a half feet (3.2 m) or seven seconds at 24 frame/s, the changeover cue should appear, which signals the projectionist to actually make the changeover. When this second cue appears, the projectionist has one and a half feet (457 mm) or one second at 24 frame/s to make the changeover - if it doesn't occur within one second, the tail black leader of the exhausted reel will be projected on the screen.

On some projectors, the operator would be alerted to the change by a bell that operated when the feed reel rotation exceeded a certain speed (that reel rotates faster as the film is exhausted), although many such projectors do not have such an auditory system. During the actual operation of a changeover, the two projectors use an interconnected electrical control connected to the changeover button so that as soon as the button is pressed, the douser on the old reel is closed in sync with the douser for the new reel. If done properly, a changeover should be virtually unnoticeable to an audience. In older theaters, there may be manually operated, sliding covers in front of the projection booth's windows. A changeover with this system is often clearly visible as a wipe on the screen.

The size of the reels can vary based on the projectors, but generally films are divided and distributed in reels of roughly 2000 feet (610 m) about 22 minutes at 24 frame/s. Some projectors can even accommodate up to 6000 feet (1,830 m), which minimizes the number of changeovers in a showing. Certain countries also divide their film reels up differently; Russian films, for example, often come on 1000 foot (305 m) reels, although it's likely that most projectionists working with changeovers would combine them into longer reels of at least 2000 feet (610 m), to minimize changeovers and also give sufficient time for threading and any possibly needed troubleshooting time.

There are two largely used single reel systems (also known as long-play systems) today: the tower system (vertical feed and takeup) and the platter system (horizontal feed and takeup). The tower system largely resembles the two reel system, except in that the tower itself is generally a separate piece of equipment used with a slightly modified standard projector. The feed and takeup reels are held vertically on the axis, except behind the projector, on oversized spools with 12,000 foot (3,660 m) capacity or about 133 minutes at 24 frame/s. This large capacity alleviates the need for a changeover on an average-length feature; all of the reels are spliced together into one giant one.

The tower is designed with four spools, two on each side, each with its own motor. This allows the whole spool to be immediately rewound after a showing; the extra two spools on the other side allow for a film to be shown while another is being rewound or even made up directly onto the tower. Each spool requires its own motor in order to set proper tensioning for the film, since it has to travel (relatively) much further between the projector film transport and the spools. As each spool gains or loses film, the tension must be periodically checked and adjusted so that the film can be transported on and off the spools without either sagging or snapping.

In a platter system the individual 20 minute reels of film are also spliced together as one large reel, but the film is then wound onto a horizontal rotating table called a platter. Three or more platters are stacked together to create a platter system. Most of the platters in a platter system will be occupied by film prints; whichever platter happens to be empty serves as the "take-up reel" to receive the film that is playing from another platter. The way the film is fed from the platter to the projector is not unlike an eight-track audio cartridge. Film is unwound from the center of the platter through a mechanism called a "brain" which controls the speed of the platter's rotation so that it matches the speed of the film as it is fed to the projector.

The film winds through a series of rollers from the platter stack to the projector, through the projector, through another series of rollers back to the platter stack, and then onto the platter serving as the take-up reel. This system makes it possible to project a film several times a day without needing to rewind it. As the projectionist threads the projector for each showing, he transfers the brain mechanism from the empty platter to the full platter and the film then plays back onto the platter it came from. In the case of a double feature, each film plays from a full platter onto an empty platter, swapping positions on the platter stack throughout the day.

The advantage of a platter is that the film isn't subjected to the stresses of being rewound each show. Rewinding risks rubbing the film against itself, which can cause scratching of the film and smearing of the emulsion which carries the pictures. The disadvantages of the platter system are that the film can acquire diagonal scratches on it if proper care is not taken while threading film from platter to projector, and the film has more opportunity to collect dust and dirt as long lengths of film are exposed to the air. A clean projection booth kept at the proper humidity is of great importance, as are cleaning devices that can remove dirt from the film print as it plays.

The single reel system can allow for the complete automation of the projection booth operations, given the proper auxiliary equipment. Since films are still transported in multiple reels they must be joined together when placed on the projector reel and taken apart when the film is to be returned to the distributor. It is the complete automation that has enabled the modern "multiplex" cinema - a single site typically containing from 16 to 24 theaters with only a few projection and sound technicians, rather than a platoon of projectionists. The multiplex also offers a great amount of flexibility to a theater operator, enabling multiple theaters to exhibit the same popular production in multiple theaters with staggered starting times.

Smooth wheels with triangular pins called sprockets engage perforations punched into one or both edges of the film stock. These serve to set the pace of film movement through the projector and any associated sound playback system. As with motion picture cameras, the intermittent motion of the gate requires that there be loops above and below the gate in order to serve as a buffer between the constant speed enforced by the sprockets above and below the gate and the intermittent motion enforced at the gate. Some projectors also have a sensitive trip pin above the gate to guard against the upper loop becoming too big. If the loop hits the pin, it will close the dousers and stop the motor to prevent an excessively large loop from jamming the projector.

A spring loaded pressure plate functions to align the film in a consistent image plane, both flat and perpendicular to the optical axis. It also provides sufficient drag to prevent film motion during the frame display, while still allowing free motion under control of the intermittent mechanism. The plate also has spring-loaded runners to help hold film while in place and advance it during motion. For smaller gauge projectors (8mm and 16 mm), a pawl mechanism engages the film's sprocket hole one side, or holes on each side. This pawl advances only when the film is to be moved to the next image. As the pawl retreats for the next cycle it is drawn back and does not engage the film. This is similar to the claw mechanism in a motion picture camera.

In 35 mm and 70 mm projectors, there usually is a special sprocket immediately underneath the pressure plate known as the intermittent sprocket. Unlike the all the other sprockets in the projector, which run continuously, the intermittent sprocket operates in tandem with the shutter, and only moves while the shutter is blocking the lamp, so that the motion of the film cannot be seen. It also moves in a discrete amount at a time, equal to the number of perforations that make up a frame (4 for 35 mm, 5 for 70 mm). The intermittent movement in these projectors is usually provided by a Maltese_Cross_mechanism. IMAX projectors use what's known as the rolling loop method, in which each frame is sucked into the gate by a vacuum, and positioned by registration pins in the perforations corresponding to that frame.

Types of Projectors

Projectors are classified by the size of the film used. Typical film sizes:

— *8 mm*: Long used for home movies before the video camera, this uses double sprocketed 16 mm film, which is run through the camera twice. The 16 mm film is then split lengthwise into two 8 mm pieces that are sliced to make a single projectable film with sprockets on one side.

— *Super 8*: Developed by Kodak this film stock uses very small sprocket holes close to the edge that allow more of the film stock to be used for the images. This increases the quality of the image. The film is premade in the 8 mm width, not split during processing as is the earlier 8 mm. Magnetic stripes could be added to carry encoded sound to be added after film development.

— *16 mm*: This was a popular format for audio-visual use in schools and as a high-end home entertainment system before the advent of broadcast television. It is also the smallest format that can carry an optically encoded sound track.

— *35 mm*: The most common film size for theatrical productions during the first half of the 20th century. In fact, the common 35 mm camera, developed by Leica was designed to use this film stock and was originally intended to be used for test shots by movie directors and cinematographers.

— *70 mm*: High end movie productions are often shot using this size and some theaters are capable of projecting it. 70 mm film is also used in both the flat and domed IMAX projection system. In IMAX the film is oriented for even more effective image area than in other formats.

Some high quality productions intended for 35 mm anamorphic release are shot in and the master prints constructed using 70 mm film stock. A 35 mm print made from a 70 mm master print is significantly better in appearance than an all 35 mm process. Regardless of the sound format, any sound represented on the film image itself will not be the sound for the particular frame it occupies. All optical sound formats must be offset from the image because the image is projected with intermittent motion. If the sound head on the projector was adjacent to the gate, the sound would be a jerky start-stop-start-stop and so on. Therefore the sound head requires continuous motion and will be located a certain number of frames before or after the gate.

With 16 mm and the larger sizes it is practical to add a narrow channel of optically encoded sound track. This is read using an illuminating light or laser and a photo-sensor solar cell. In 16 mm, this is a single mono track, and the sound head is 26 frames after the gate. In 35 mm, this can be mono or stereo, the latter including several different Dolby sound matrixing systems (including Dolby A and Dolby SR). The sound head is located twenty frames after the gate for 35 mm projectors. Originally optical sound was variable density, where the transparency/ opacity level of the sound track was used to represent sound. This had disadvantages because the grain of the fill caused a background hiss, and so was replaced with the now-universal standard variable area. In this system, a clear waveform on black background represents the sound, and the width of the waveform is equivalent to the amplitude. Variable area does have slightly less frequency response than variable density, it should be noted.

Digital Sound

Modern theatrical systems use optical representations of digitally encoded multi-channel sound. An advantage of digital systems is that the offset between the sound and picture heads can be varied and then set with the digital processors. Digital sound heads are usually above the gate. All digital sound systems currently in use have the ability to instantly and virtually imperceptibly fall back to the optical sound system should the digital data be corrupt or the whole system fail.

Cinema Digital Sound (CDS): Created by Kodak and ORC (Optical Radiation Corporation), Cinema Digital Sound was the first attempt to bring multi-channel digital sound to first-run theaters. CDS was available on both 35 mm and 70 mm films. Film prints equipped with CDS did not have the conventional analog optical or magnetic soundtracks to serve as a "back-up" in case the digital sound was unreadable. Another disadvantage of not having an analog back-up track is that Cinema Digital Sound (CDS) required extra film prints be made for the theaters equipped to play CDS. The three formats that followed, Dolby Digital, DTS and SDDS, can co-exist with each other and the analog optical soundtrack on a single version of the film print. This means that a film print carrying all three of these formats (and the analog optical format, usually Dolby SR) can be played in whichever format the theater is equipped to handle. CDS did not achieve wide-spread use and ultimately failed. It premiered with the film Dick Tracy and was used with several other films, such as Days of Thunder and Terminator 2: Judgement Day.

Sony Dynamic Digital Stereo (SDDS) : SDDS sound runs on the outside of 35 mm film, between the perforations and the edges, on both edges of the film. It is the only digital system that can handle up to eight tracks of sound. The additional two tracks are for an extra pair of screen channels (Left Center and Right Center) located between the 3 regular screen channels (Left, Center and Right). A pair of CCD's located in a unit above the projector read the two SDDS tracks. The information is decoded and decompressed before being passed along to a Sony cinema sound processor, which means it can be equalized in the digital domain. In contrast, DTS and Dolby Digital soundtracks both are passed through to standard analog Dolby cinema sound processors which are also used for analog optical sound, so equalization of the sound is only analog. The digital compression of SDDS is better than DTS, but inferior to Dolby Digital. SDDS premiered with the film The Last Action Hero.

Dolby Digital : Also known to enthusiasts as Spectral Recording Digital or "SR-D." Sound is printed between the perforations and is 26 frames before the picture (the offset can be varied based on processing presets). It can handle up to six tracks, and has the best compression of the digital formats. The images between each perforation are read by a CCD located either above the projector or in the regular analog sound head below the film gate. The information is then decoded, decompressed, and converted to analog by an SR-D processor before going to a standard Dolby analog multi-format cinema sound processor. A consumer version of Dolby Digital is also used on most DVD's, often at higher data rates than the original film. Dolby Digital officially premiered with the film Batman Returns, but it was earlier tested at some screenings of Star Trek: The Undiscovered Country.

Digital Theater Systems (DTS): DTS actually stores the sound information on separate CD-ROMs supplied with the film. The CDs are fed into a special modified computer (usually a 386 or 486 system) which syncs up with the film through the use of DTS time code, decompresses the sound, and passes it through to a standard analog Dolby processor. The time code is placed between the optical sound tracks and the actual picture, and is read by an optical LED ahead of the gate. The time code is actually the only sound system which is not offset within the film from the picture, but still needs to be physically set offset ahead of the gate in order to maintain continuous motion.

Each disc can hold slightly over two hours of sound, so longer films will require a second disc, which means that the sound will temporarily revert back to the optical track while changing discs. DTS is a six track system (although it has an earlier, discontinued four track counterpart), and as might be expected of the oldest of the three digital systems, has the most inferior compression. Of the three digital formats currently in use, DTS is the only one that has been used with 70 mm presentations. DTS was premiered on Jurassic Park. A consumer version of DTS is available on some DVD's.

Magnetic Sound

70 mm, which had no optical sound, used the 5 millimeters gained between the 65 mm negative and the final release print to place three magnetic tracks on each side of the perforations, for a total of six tracks. Unlike all other non-double head magnetic sound, 70 mm magnetic heads are located before the gate. Until the introduction of digital sound, it was fairly common for 35 mm films to be blown up to 70 mm often just to take advantage of the greater number of sound tracks. 35 mm four-track magnetic sound was used from the 1950s through the mid 1970s for big-budget feature prints. It was of excellent quality, although somewhat prone to damage and erasure over time.

Analog optical stereo gained popularity (it was also more durable and far less expensive to include on a film print), 35 mm four-track magnetic sound was increasingly only used for special road show screenings, and the development of digital sound systems made it completely obsolete. 35 mm and 16 mm each are sometimes run in sync with a separate reel of magnetic sound (known as double head projection because two reels are running on one projector in sync); the image goes through a gate while the magnetic reel passes over a sound head. Since the sound is on a separate reel, it does not need to be offset from the image. This system is usually used only for very low-budget or student productions, or for screening rough cuts of films before the creation of a final married print.

Sync between the two reels is checked with SMPTE Academy leader, also known as countdown leader. If the two reels are synced, there should be one frame of "plop" sound exactly on the "3" frame of the countdown. On certain stocks of Super 8 and 16 mm it an iron-oxide sound recording strip was added for the direct synchronous recording of sound which could then be played by projectors with a magnetic sound head. It has since been discontinued by Kodak on both gauges.

Lenses and Screens

Orthographic : Before the advent of certain wide screen technologies, lenses always reproduced the exact proportions of the film image onto the screen. Such lenses are relatively simple to design and manufacture. Prior to modern wide screen, the industry standard image ratio of width to height was 4:3. 35 mm VistaVision was a wide screen orthographic system. The wide image was obtained by running the film horizontally across the gate so that the width limitation of the film was transformed to a height limitation.

Anamorphic : The 1950's saw the development of wide screen films using special lenses for filming and projection. The images on these films retained the same proportions as in the earlier films (a 4:3 width to height ratio). The wide image is compressed onto the film in the camera using additional cylindrical elements within the lens, with a corresponding lens used in the projector to expand the image to the wide screen. This technique is called anamorphic projection and various implementations have been marketed under several brand names, including CinemaScope, Panavision and Superscope, with Technirama implementing a slightly different anamorphic technique using vertical expansion to the film rather than horizontal compression.

Of the anamorphic methods, arguably the best image was produced by the Todd-AO (for Michael Todd and American Optical) using 70 mm film and a large, curved screen. Around the World in Eighty Days starring David Niven and Cantinflas was the leading general release production using this process. A popular film recently released (2004) as a remake, the original was also released as a Cinemascope print, by comparison to the Todd-AO original as watching television is to being in a movie theater. Similar 70 mm processes include Super (and Ultra) Panavision and VistaVision.

The IMAX® dome projection method (called "OMNIMAX®") uses 70 mm film oriented to maximize the image area and extreme wide angle lenses to obtain an almost hemispherical image. The field of view is tilted, as is the projection hemisphere, so one may view a portion of the ground in the foreground. Owing to the great area covered by the picture it is not as bright as seen with flat screen projection, but the immersive qualities are quite convincing. While there are not many theaters capable of displaying this format there are regular productions in the fields of nature, travel, science, and history, and productions may be viewed in most U.S. large urban regions. These dome theaters are mostly located in large and prosperous science and technology museums.

The IMAX® flat screen system uses large format film, a wide and deep screen, and close and quite steep "stadium" seating. The effect is to fill the visual field to a greater degree than is possible with conventional wide screen systems. Like the IMAX® dome, this is found in major urban areas, but unlike the dome system it is practical to reformat existing movie releases to this method. Also, the geometry of the theater and screen are more amenable to inclusion within a newly constructed but otherwise conventional multiple theater complex than is the dome style theater.

One wide screen development during the 1950's used non-anamorphic projection, but used three side by side synchronised projectors. Called Cinerama, the images were projected onto an extremely wide, curved screen. Some seams were said to be visible between the images but the almost complete filling of the visual field made up for this. This showed some commercial success as a limited location (only in major cities) exhibition of the technology in This is Cinerama, but the only memorable story-telling film of two made for this technology was How the West Was Won, widely seen only in its Cinemascope re-release.

While neither a technical nor a commercial success, the business model survives as implemented by the documentary production, limited release locations, and long running exhibitions of IMAX® dome movies. A slide projector is an opto-mechanical device to view photographic slides. It has four main elements: a fan-cooled electric light bulb or other light source, a reflector and "condensing" lens to direct the light to the slide, a holder for the slide and a focusing lens. Light passes through the transparent slide and lens, and the resulting image is enlarged and projected onto a perpendicular flat screen so the audience can view its reflection. Alternatively the image may be projected onto a translucent "rear projection" screen, often used for continuous automatic display for close viewing.

Stock photography is photography or other imagery of common landmarks, concepts, and events that can be used and reused for commercial design purposes. Book publishers, specialty publishers, magazines, advertising agencies, film makers, web designers, graphic artists, interior decor firms, corporate creative groups, and other entities utilize stock photography to fulfill the needs of their creative assignments. By using stock photography instead of hiring a photographer to perform on location shooting, customers can save valuable time and stay on budget. With a wealth of images, stock photography databases that may be searched online save photo researchers valuable time when they are looking for just the right image.

Today's digital delivery methods, images may be purchased online and delivered via FTP or email, the very same day. Stock photography is sometimes called a photo archive, or just stock photos. The term photo archive often refers to the website or physical location where the photographs are stored. Photo archives are also sometimes called image banks. As modern stock photography distributors often carry stills, video, and illustrations, none of the existing terminology provides a perfect match for the state of the industry.

8

Digital Photography

Digital photography, as opposed to film photography, uses an electronic sensor to record the image as a piece of electronic data rather than as chemical changes on film. There are two main types of sensors:

— charge-coupled device (CCD)

— CMOS semiconductor sensor

There are also two main types of sensor mechanisms:

— Area array

— Linear array (very rare, only limited to the highest-end)

An area array sensor reads the entire image plane at once, whereas a linear array sensor works more like a flatbed scanner. Since this technology predates area arrays, it was available earlier, in professionally-priced cameras. With the advent of area array sensors, consumer digital cameras became available for considerably lower prices. Except for some linear array type at the highest-end and web cams at the lowest-end, a digital memory device (usually flash memory; floppy disks and CD-RWs are less common) is usually used for storing images, which may then be transferred to a computer later. Many linear array type cameras and web cams connect directly to a computer.

The advantages of digital photography over traditional film include:

— Instant review of pictures, with no wait for the film to be developed: if there's a problem with a picture, you find out immediately and can correct the problem and take another picture.

— You only pay for the printing of successful pictures.

— Colour reproduction and gamut is not dependent on film quality.

— Permanent storage on digital media is considerably cheaper than film.

— There's no need to scan the picture before using it in a computer.

— Digital cameras can be smaller and lighter than film cameras of equivalent quality.

— Image quality does not degrade with time.

Recent digital cameras from leading manufacturers such as Nikon and Canon have promoted the adoption of digital Single-lens reflex cameras (SLRs) by photojournalists. Images captured at 2+ megapixels are deemed to be of sufficient quality for small images in newspaper or magazine reproduction.

Six megapixel images, found in modern digital SLRs, when combined with high-end lenses can match or even exceed the detail of film prints taken with 35 mm film based SLRs, and the latest 12-megapixel models can produce astoundingly detailed images better than almost all 35mm images. Some professional models can capture 20- to 40-megapixel images. These ultra high resolution pictures may not be very useful to ordinary users, but they are useful to artists, scientists and commercial uses.

Advantages of Film

- Film cameras are quicker to use: you don't have to wait for the camera to start up, for the photosensor to capture the image, or for the picture to be compressed and saved to the memory card.
- Batteries last much longer in film cameras.
- Film camera batteries are of standard types and are easier to replace.
- A digital camera's LCD may become unusable in very bright light.
- Image noise, a major problem of digital cameras, is no issue with conventional film.
- The user does not need to know how to handle a computer.
- A picture on film is likely to last longer than a harddisk or CD-R used to store digital pictures.

A typical digital camera's aspect ratio is 1.33 (4:3). The same ratio as today's NTSC or PAL/SECAM TVs or earliest movies. However, a 35 mm picture's aspect ratio is 1.5 (3:2). If you send your digital pictures to a lab to print, either the top and bottom parts of your pictures will be gone, or you will see ugly blanks on the right and left edges.

The quality of a digital image is the sum of various factors. Pixel count (typically listed in megapixels) is only one of the major factors, though it's the most heavily marketed.

1. Analog
   - Lens quality
     - Lens resolution

  - Geometric distortion
  - Color dispersion
  - Inner reflection
- — CCD/CMOS noise

2. Digital
   - — Data gathering
     - Pixel count
     - Color depth
     - Bayer filter calculation (for cameras with Bayer filter sensors)
     - Color correction
   - — Data storage
     - File format

Pixel Counts

The number of pixels n for a given maximum resolution (w horizontal pixels by h vertical pixels) can be found using the formula: n = wh. This yields e. g. 1.92 megapixels for an image of 1600 x 1200. The majority of digital cameras have a 4:3 aspect ratio, i.e. w/h = 4/3. The megapixel or pixel count quoted by the manufacturers is misleading because it is not truly representative of the number of full colour pixels. For cameras using a Bayer sensor it is the number of single coloured photosites (light sensitive areas) on the sensor. For the Foveon X3 sensor the number currently (Feb 2004 - Sigma SD-10) presented by Sigma is the number of photosites times three (multiplied because each photosite records three colours), however the images that result will have a number of pixels equivalent to the number of photosites - not the tripled number quoted.

It is not possible to directly compare the megapixel ratings of these two sensors but in many people's opinions a 6MP Bayer filter sensor is roughly equivalent to a 10.2MP Foveon X3 (3.4MP*3). Some hold the opinion that the Foveon is worse than this and the ratio is more like one Bayer to two Foveon. It is largely a matter of personal opinion so prints from the two sensors should be inspected by interested parties.

With the acceptable image quality and the other advantages of digital photography (particularly the time pressures, of vital importance to daily newspapers) an increasing number of professional news photographers use these devices. It has also been adopted by many amateur snapshot photographers, who take advantage of the convenience of the form when sending images by email and to place on the World Wide Web. Some commercial photographers, and some amateurs interested in artistic photography, tend to avoid digital photography at this stage, as they believe that the image quality available from a digital camera of a given price is still inferior to that available from a film camera, and the quality of images taken on medium format film is near-impossible to match at any price with a digital camera.

Some have expressed a concern that changing computer technology may make digital photographs inaccessible in the future while printed images have a very long lifespan. A related concern in a specialised application is the use of digital photographs in court proceedings, with the perceived difficulty of demonstrating an image's authenticity. Other commercial photographers, and many amateurs, have enthusiastically embraced digital photography, as they believe that its flexibility and lower long-term costs outweigh its initial price disadvantages. Almost all of the cost of digital photography is capital cost, meaning that the cost is for the equipment needed to store and copy the images, and once purchased requires virtually no further expense outlay.

Film photography requires continuous expenditure of (much higher amounts of) funds for supplies and developing. Digital photography was used in astronomy long before its use by the general public and had almost completely displaced photographic plates by the early 1980s. Not only are CCDs more sensitive to light than plates, but the information can be downloaded onto a computer for data analysis. The CCDs used in astronomy are similar to those used by the general public, but are cooled to liquid nitrogen temperatures so as to reduce the noise which is caused by heat.

In late 2002, 2 megapixel cameras were available in the United States for less than $100, with some 1 megapixel cameras for under $60. At the same time, many discount stores with photo labs introduced a "digital front end," allowing consumers to obtain true chemical prints (as opposed to ink-jet prints) in an hour. These prices competed with prints from negatives. In July 2003, digital cameras entered the "single-use" market with the release of the Ritz Dakota Digital, a 1.2 megapixel (1280x960) CMOS-based digital camera costing only $11 (USD).

Following the familiar single-use concept long in use with film cameras, the Dakota Digital was intended to be used by a consumer one time only, be returned to the store, and the consumer would receive back prints and a CD with the digital photos, but not the camera (The camera gets refurbished and resold). Since the introduction of the Dakota Digital, a handful of similar single-use digital cameras have appeared, most of which are functionally identical to the original Dakota Digital, and others that have superior specifications, such as higher resolutions and LCD displays that show the previous picture taken. Most, if not all, of these single-use digital cameras cost less than $20 (USD), not including processing.

Kodak announced in January 2004 that they would no longer sell Kodak-branded film cameras in the developed world, an indication that the transition to digital photography for amateurs is well underway. The technology was improving so rapidly that one camera already went out of production before it was awarded "camera of the year" award. Nowadays, sales of digital cameras are more than triple those of traditional film cameras.

Exchangeable image file format (Exif) is a set of file formats specified for use in digital cameras. This specifies the use of TIFF for the highest quality format and JPEG as a space-saving but lower quality format. Many low-end cameras can deliver only JPEG files. Another format that may be encountered is CCD-RAW, which is unstandardised. A large variety of data storage device formats are used in consumer digital cameras:

— Secure Digital Card (SD)

— Compact Flash (CF-I and CF-II)

— Memory Stick

— Multi Media Card (MMC)

— SmartMedia

— xD-Picture Card (xD)

— USB keydrive

Most digital cameras are built to operate as a self-contained unit. This is especially so at the lower-end, for these cameras usually include zoom lens and flashes that cannot be changed. However, at the highest-end, some digital cameras are nothing but a sophisticated light-sensing unit. Experienced photographers attach these digital "camera backs" to their professional medium format SLR cameras, such as a Hasselblad.

— Area array

  - CCD

  - CMOS

— Linear array

  - CCD (monochrome)

  - 3-strip CCD with color filters

Digital cameras have tossed many novices into the deep end of the photographic pool, with the result that learning how to shoot good pictures has been a sink-or-swim affair. Few have grounded their digital knowledge in traditional film basics, like lens length and light metering. It's time to catch up.

Remember the early days of desktop publishing, when graphic design novices suddenly found themselves (either by choice or assignment) taking on layout and design jobs? Digital technology is having a similar effect on photography.

Because of the low cost and extreme convenience of digital photography, many people are being cast in the role of photographer when it comes time to update the company Web site or newsletter, or take some simple product shots. Granted, in an ideal world, these jobs should be going to a professional photographer. Outside the workplace, people with no previous photography experience are picking up digital cameras and finding them very compelling. Browse through any of the popular photoblogging sites on the Net, and you'll find lots of entries from people who comment "I'd never really taken any pictures before I got my digital camera," and now they're posting photos — in some cases, extremely good photos.

Because of the automatic features and ease-of-use of the modern digital camera (and point-and-shoot film camera) it's easy to pick up a digital camera and take decent pictures without having to learn some of the important, basic concepts that older technology forced beginning photographers to learn. Over the next two installments of this column, we're going to look at some of the basic photographic concepts and principles that experienced film photographers take for granted, but that the digital photographer, might never have learned. These principles should help you get better results from your camera, and perhaps help you better understand the creative possibilities at your disposal.

These days, almost all digital cameras come with zoom lenses. We're talking about actual optical zoom lenses, not digital zoom features. The great thing about a zoom lens is that, for small cameras with fixed lenses, a zoom gives you a choice of focal lengths, while for cameras with interchangeable lenses, they enable you to carry less gear. Inexperienced photographers, though, don't necessarily know that a zoom lens is not just a way to get closer to a distant subject. In addition to allowing you to gain a telephoto view of a distant object, your zoom lens provides you with a rather profound control of the sense of space in your scene. Zooming can also — intentionally or not — create some rather weird distortions of your subject.

Most people assume that the automatic light meter in their camera calculates the best possible exposure for a scene, and in most cases this is true. However, there are times when your light meter will merely do an adequate job. Understanding some light meter fundamentals will help. The goal of a light meter is to calculate a shutter speed and aperture value (and, in some digital cameras, an ISO speed) that will yield a good image. Light meters vary in their approach to solving this problem. Simple systems take basic luminance measurements, while high-end meters measure brightness from many parts of the image, and compare this information to a database of correctly exposed images to come up with a proper exposure.

In general, though, you should remember the following two things about your light meter: It knows nothing about color, and it assumes that you're pointing it at a scene that is 18% gray. If that last item seems a little arbitrary, you're just going to have to take it on faith. The fact is: Most scenes reflect about 18% of the light that strikes them, meaning that if the camera assumes it's looking at a scene that's 18% gray, and calculates an exposure accordingly, then that exposure is probably going to be valid for your particular scene.

Since most scenes truly are 18% gray, then your meter's assumption is usually valid. However, if you're standing in a field of snow, taking a picture of an albino in a white parka who's listening to an iPod, then your light meter's fundamental assumption is going to be wrong. The result will be an image of an ashen figure wearing a dirty parka while listening to an unidentifiable MP3 player, because the light meter will have correctly calculated a reading that renders the scene as gray.

Similarly, if you're shooting a Johnny Cash impersonator standing on a lava flow holding a bowling ball, then following your light meter's suggestion is going to result in the tones in your image being rendered as gray rather than black. For these instances, you'll need to out-think your light meter and over- or under-expose to render tones correctly. Over-expose to render white objects white, under-expose to darken black objects. The easiest way to do this is with your camera's exposure compensation controls, though you can also use any manual exposure modes that your camera might have.

Colors also have a luminance value. A deep red color, for example, might have a luminance value that is darker than 18% gray and so will be rendered more accurately and more richly with an underexposure. One of the great advantages of digital over film is expense (or lack thereof). If you're not sure whether you need to over- or underexpose, then bracket your shots. Shoot one at the meter's recommendation, then some additional frames over- and under. Many cameras offer auto-bracketing features that, when combined with the camera's burst or drive mode, will automatically shoot a series of bracketed shots. Later, you can examine the images to decide which yields the most accurate exposure for your subject.

The concerns presented here are nothing that photographers haven't always faced. However, with a digital camera, it's easy to shoot pictures without learning these concepts ahead of time. Hopefully, understanding these concerns a little better will help you to shoot better pictures.

— Single-shot

— Multi-shot (three-shot, usually)

These camera backs are originally used only in a studio to take pictures of still objects. Most earlier digital camera backs were using linear array sensors which could take seconds or even minutes for a complete high-resolution scan. The linear array sensor acts like its counterpart used in a flatbed image scanner by moving vertically to digitize the image. Many of these cameras could only capture grayscale images. To take a color picture, it requires three separate scans done with a rotating colored filter. These are called multi-shot backs. Some other camera backs are using CCD arrays similar to typical cameras. These are called single-shot backs.

Since it is much easier to manufacture a high-quality linear CCD array that has only thousands pixels than a CCD matrix that has millions of them, very high resolution linear CCD camera backs were available much earlier than their CCD matrix counterparts. For example, you could buy an expensive camera back with an over 7,000-pixel horizontal resolution in the mid-1990s. However, as of 2004, you can still hardly buy a comparable CCD matrix camera of the same resolution.

Many modern digital camera backs are using very large CCD matrices. This eliminated the need of scanning. For example, Fujifilm produces a 20-million-pixel digital camera back with a 52 mm x 37 mm (2.04" x 1.45") CCD in 2003. This CCD array is a little smaller than a frame of 120 film and much larger than a 35 mm frame (36 mm x 24 mm). In comparison, a consumer digital camera usually uses an itsy-bitsy so-called 1/2.5" or 7.176 mm x 5.329 mm (so-called 1/1.8") CCD sensor. Beware, the 1/2.5" or 1/ 1.8" diagonal measurement is the size of the entire CCD chip. The actual photo-sensitive area is much smaller.

A digital camera back is a good idea to smooth the transition from film to digital. A photographer can reuse his beloved SLR camera and lens without much trouble. To some medium format camera users, the convienence of a bellows has no substitute. However, there's a catch. Only a few very expensive high-end digital cameras or camera backs could use film-sized CCDs. Since a camera back's CCD is seldom as large as the film it replaces, either one has to use a smaller CCD, or to use multiple smaller CCDs that form a larger piece. For example, various cameras of the late 1990s based on the "building block" CCDs of Philips use of four to six 12 x 12 mm 1-megapixel CCDs to form larger light sensors.

If a smaller sensor is used, the focal length of the lens shall be adjusted to the actual size of the CCD. For example, when you're using a 35 mm SLR camera with a standard 50 mm lens and a 4/3" digital camera back with a 18.0 mm x 13.5 mm CCD (about half as wide as a 35 mm frame), your 50 mm normal lens becomes a 100 mm telephoto lens. If you want a 50 mm lens, you have to buy a 25 mm wide-angle lens. Digital imaging or digital image acquisition is the creation of digital images, typically from a physical object. The term is often assumed to imply or include the processing, compression, storage, printing, and display of such images.

A digital image may be created directly from a physical scene by a camera or similar device. Alternatively, it may be obtained from another image in an analog medium, like photographs, photographic film, or printed paper, by a scanner or similar device. Many technical images — such as those acquired with tomographic equipment, side-looking radar, or radio telescopes — are actually obtained by complex processing of non-image data. Finally, a digital image can also be computed from a geometric model or mathematical formula.

The Digital Revolution started in the last decades of the 20th century. It was a transition from the storage of information on fixed material objects dedicated to specific purposes (books for words, phonograph records or audio cassettes for sound, film for images), to the storage of all information in a binary digital format, which is readily stored on a variety of media. Of equal importance to the revolution was the ability to easily move the digital information between media, and to access or distribute it remotely.

Underlying the digital revolution was the development of the digital electronic computer, the personal computer, and particularly of the microprocessor which enabled computer technology to be embedded into a huge range of objects from cameras to personal music players. Equally important was the development of transmission technologies including computer networking, the Internet and digital broadcasting.

While there have been huge benefits to the digital revolution, especially in terms of the accessibility of information, there are a number of concerns. For those living in the present, the digital revolution has ushered in an new age of mass surveillance, generating a range of new civil and human rights issues. From the perspective of the historian, a large part of our history is known through physical objects from the past that have been found or preserved, particularly in written documents. Although digital information is easily created, it is also fragile and easily deleted or destroyed.

Changes in storage formats can make recovery of data difficult or near impossible, as can the storage of information on obsolete media for which reproduction equipment is unavailable, and even identifying what such data is and whether it is of interest can be near impossible if it no longer easily readable, or if there is a large number of such files to identify. These problems are further compounded by the use of digital rights management and other copy protection technologies which, being designed to only allow the data to be read on specific machines, may well make future data recovery impossible. Interestingly, the Voyager Golden Record, which is intended to be read by an intelligent extraterrestrial (perhaps a suitable parallel to a human from the distant future), is recorded in analog rather than digital format specifically for easy interpretation and analysis.

9

Literacy Journalism

Journalists employ many approaches and styles when they are writing a story. Sometimes they employ techniques of the storyteller. They attempt to communicate the facts in an artful manner. This approach grew from what used to be called "new journalism" in the 1960s and 70s, and is now referred to as literary journalism. It is evident in the range of styles found in contemporary newspapers and magazines.

Learning Objectives

Students will:

— recognize writing as a process of constructing meaning for themselves and others

— relate the structure of the work to the author's purposes and theme

— recognize the importance for journalists of interviewing, researching, and reporting

— identify the characteristics of new journalism and literary journalism

— experiment with literary journalism.

Activities

— New journalism was a term that was used when critics and writers became aware of a new style of journalism in the 1960s. In his book, The New Journalism, Tom Wolfe describes a trend whereby nonfiction writers adopted the techniques of realist novelists to bring power to their stories. He cited the four following techniques as ones that brought about significant changes in journalistic writing:

a) *Scene-by-scene construction*: Writers told their stories by moving from scene to scene rather than reporting only historical facts. They sought to bring the people involved to life for the reader, so the reader could experience the human context of the story.

b) *Use of dialogue*: The primary way of creating character was the inclusion of dialogue. Wolfe says that realistic dialogue involves the reader more than any other device, and that dialogue defines character more quickly than any other means.

c) *Use of third person point of view*: Scenes were presented to the reader through the eyes of a particular character, so that readers could feel as though they were inside the character's mind and could understand his or her actions and emotions. This technique meant that the journalist had to do exhaustive, first-hand research.

d) *The recording of everyday details*: Wolfe says that the details of everyday life were once considered irrelevant in journalism, but that the writers of so-called new journalism understood that these details could be symbolic and contribute to social understanding. According to Wolfe, the recording of such details as habits, customs, attitudes, clothing, and food contributes to an understanding of a person's "life status" or beliefs about his or her position in the world.

— Have students examine the journalistic styles of the 1960s and 1070s (i.e., new journalism or "gonzo" journalism). They might consider the work of Tom Wolfe or Hunter S. Thompson. What is particularly effective in their work? How does the style fit the subject matter? What is not effective? Why?

— Since the 1970s the criteria that define literary journalism have changed, and the inclusion of fictional writing techniques is now only one of several defining criteria. In her book The Art of Fact, Barbara Lounsberry lists the following as the characteristics of literary nonfiction:

a) Documentable subject matter chosen from the real world rather than the writer's imagination.

Anything in the natural world is subject matter for the literary nonfiction writer. The following are examples:

— the lives of individuals (e.g., one person's struggle)

— human institutions (e.g., government)

— cultural groups (e.g., country music fans)

— events (e.g., current events)

— the natural world (e.g., environmental stories).

— Exhaustive research.

In order to bring the full world of the stories alive, the writer must conduct extensive research and be able to verify every detail.

The scene: Lounsberry says that the scene is a necessary element in making a story "artful". Instead of reporting on a story, the writer of literary nonfiction recasts the story so that it has life and depth.

Fine writing and literary prose style: Writing cannot be literary without attention to language. Literary writers must be in complete control of their use of language, whatever their prose preferences are.

In his book, The Literary Journalists, Norman Sims contends that the change in journalism came about as writers began to see private lives rather than dominant institutions as sources of information. He says that literary journalists saw the need to immerse themselves in complex subjects in order to establish their own perspective and authority, so that they could do more than simply report the facts as presented to them. Sims gives the following as characteristics of literary journalism:

Immersion: Literary journalists invest a great deal of time and effort learning about their subject. They usually begin with an emotional connection to the subject, and then immerse themselves in learning everything they can about the world of the subject and the people involved.

Structure: Literary journalists believe the same about structure that fiction writers do: structure contributes to meaning. Therefore, structure is not simply linear. It is carefully controlled by the writer and is unique to each project. Where a portion of the story is placed, and what it is placed next to, will profoundly affect the meaning the reader constructs as he or she is engaged with the story.

Accuracy: The ethical commitment to accuracy has not changed with the advent of literary journalism. If a writer wishes to adopt a voice of authority on a subject, then he or she must be knowledgeable and present accurate information. Dialogue, for example, can not be invented. If real people speak, then the dialogue must be direct quotation.

Voice: Sims says there is no one voice that defines contemporary literary journalism. One writer might use a first person voice, where he or she is very much a part of the story. Another might remove himself or herself from the story and concentrate on the subject's own reality. The commonality is that all literary journalists consider voice a factor in what they do, and struggle to find the right voice for their story.

Responsibility: Literary journalists who often immerse themselves in people's lives and develop personal relationships with their subjects, must recognize that they have a responsibility to themselves and their subjects when the writing becomes public. Although there are no easy answers regarding what is ethical to make public, writers do have a responsibility to let their subjects know what they are doing in their research and why. Because of the subjectivity of much literary journalism, responsibility, purpose, and consequences are things the literary journalist considers.

10

Ethics and Journalism

Journalists try to follow the law and meet the ethical standards that guide their work. They are expected to be objective and accurate, to tell the truth, and to be fair. Their emphasis is usually on good taste and accurate attribution.

Learning Objectives

Students will:

- speak to clarify and extend thinking
- recognize a speaker's attitude, tone, and bias
- analyze and evaluate their own and others' writing
- evaluate the quality and reliability of various forms and examples of journalism
- state and evaluate an author's theme, tone, and viewpoint
- recognize the importance for journalists of researching, interviewing, and reporting
- understand the rights and responsibilities of the press
- understand the legal limitations on the media
- understand the limitations that may be imposed on student journalists, depending on school policy

— understand the concepts of libel and slander

— understand the concepts of stereotyping and ethnocentricism

— evaluate the concept of objectivity.

Activities for Students

— Have students consider: What is meant by "freedom of the press"? What are, or should be, limitations on freedom of the press, if any?

— Have students consider the ethics of news reporting. What role do censorship, individual privacy, libel, obscenity, pressure groups, profanity, promotion, unpopular viewpoints, sensationalism, and controversial or taboo topics play in the news? Assume that a seventeen-year-old student has been involved in a serious crime. What do they think should be reported to the public about the accused? About the victim(s)? What elements of a code of ethics affect their decision?

— Have students examine the Code of Ethics of the Society of Professional Journalists and the Canadian Press Style Book. What are the ethical standards for journalists? What is the difference between libel and slander? Encourage students to examine several editorials and identify sections that might be vulnerable to these charges. Ask students to create their own student code of ethics.

— In a pluralistic society, it is important for journalists to be inclusive of all cultural groups and to present various perspectives fairly and in a balanced and accurate manner. They should avoid stereotyping and tokenism, and focus on the merits and achievements of all peoples. Have students review reporting about various minority groups in Saskatchewan newspapers and magazines. Can they come to any conclusions about the types of stories, number of stories, quality of the reporting, presence or absence of bias, etc.? Research guidelines for equitable and bias-free reporting. As a class, develop a style sheet. Have students compare several published news stories to their own style sheet. How do they rate?

— Have students review a newspaper or magazine produced by a minority group (e.g, The Indigenous Times or Indigenous Women). On what issues or events do these publications focus? Is there a difference, depending on the publication? If so, how do they differ? Are there stories or points of view in these publications that would not be found in a mainstream newspaper? Why or why not? Is there a difference in purpose between a mainstream publication and one published by a special interest group? Is there a difference in the type of journalism?

— Have students consider the following questions: What privileges should a journalist have? What obligations and responsibilities? Should a high school journalism student have the same privileges as a paid professional? Who should be the final authority to determine what appears in a newspaper? In a student newspaper?

— "Newspeak" is language that distorts, confuses, or hides reality. Journalists must be careful how they use the language. News items should be devoid of clichés, illogical structures, and meaningless or redundant words. Have students survey a week's issues of a daily newspaper and find examples of "newspeak".

— A significant percentage of news that appears in the main section of many newspapers is crime (e.g., robberies, murders, arsons). Have students consider the following: Should crime be reported? How? What effect does this type of story have on the readers? Do people enjoy this? Is reading about crime a form of entertainment? Do you approve? How should these stories be written?

— Ask students to consider what stories their principal or teachers might censor. On what grounds?

— Ethnocentrism refers to the view that one's own race, culture, or group is inherently superior, or that the dominant culture's way of looking at something is the only way. Ethnocentrism is often very subtle, and it is difficult to detect in our own attitudes because we take the way we see the world for granted. Have students decide on several issues that might be looked at in different ways (e.g., use of the environment, child care, care of the elderly). How might these be looked at th rough different eyes? How might ethnocentrism affect news story reporting? Examine various news stories in mainstream publications for examples. The "Letters to the Editor" section of the newspaper might be a good place to look for viewpoints affected by ethnocentrism.

— The press is often accused of sensationalizing or "hyping" events. It is also accused of failing to tell the whole story, of biased or unfair reporting, and of lacking accuracy. Ask students to consider if these accusations are fair. What evidence would they use to support their stand?

— Have students consider if it is ever possible for journalists to present completely factual, objective stories if they are reporting first-hand experiences, or even if they have thoroughly researched a story. Is it fair, in certain stories, for journalists to act as interpreters as well as "reporters"? What ethical standards might guide their work?

— Critics worry about the use of media formats that blur the distinction between entertainment and news. Some accuse "tabloids" of setting the agenda for major newspapers and television networks. Have students consider if there is evidence of this and who should set the agenda.

— Some analysts believe that the news media serve three important functions with regard tc government:

a) gatekeeper—deciding which new stories will get attention

b) watchdog—reporting mismanagement, waste, and criminal activity

c) scorekeeper—making judgements about policies, legislation, and politicians.

Ask students to find examples of each of these functions in the various kinds of news coverage.

— Press councils act as independent, self-regulatory bodies to adjudicate complaints against media outlets. These councils attempt to deal with complaints against an outlet or a reporter in the gathering and publishing of news, opinion, or advertis ing. Students might explore how press councils work and what issues and complaints might go to a press council. Does Saskatchewan have a press council? What are the policies of the Canadian Association of Broadcasters?

— As more news information is internationalized and more media mergers occur, critics are concerned about media ownership and the lack of journalistic integrity. Have students consider: Who supplies the news? Who owns the media outlets? What if one company in Canada owned all the newspapers? Could journalistic integrity be lost?

EDITORIAL WRITING

The editorial writer of a newspaper and the commentator on radio or television specialize in commenting on and giving their interpretations of current events, ideas, or conditions. They express an opinion.

Learning Objectives

Students will:

— speak to share thoughts, opinions, and feelings

— present their point of view in a written work

— assess an author's ideas and techniques

— recognize the importance for journalists of researching, interviewing, and reporting

— understand the role of the editorial

— recognize various types and functions of editorial material

— write effective editorials

— identify the components of the editorial page.

Activities for Students

— Have students examine an editorial page from two large dailies and two weeklies. What are the typical elements of an editorial page? How does it differ from the front page? What is the opinion expressed in each editorial? Who stands to benefit from the opinion expressed? Who stands to lose? What facts does the editorial writer use to support the opinion? How does the writer attempt to persuade readers?

— Have students brainstorm ideas for editorials. They might consider the following purposes of editorials:

a) interpretative (explain or interpret a news event)

b) critical (criticize existing conditions and try to persuade readers to make specific changes)

c) commemorative/special occasion (mark an occasion and note its significance)

d) humorous/satirical (make fun of or criticize an event or situation).

— Have students write editorials to illustrate three of these purposes using the following format:

a) summary and background

b) stance

c) solution

d) evidence supporting stance (include the other side or opposing viewpoints if appropriate)

e) conclusion (a solid punchline).

— Editorials are meant to influence people's actions. Have students find something in their school or community that they would like to change. They should research why things are the way they are and what solutions might exist. Then, have students write a 250-300 word editorial to tell others what the problem is and what should be done.

— The editorial cartoon is sometimes the only art on an editorial page. A cartoon is an appropriate expression of opinions. Have students view different styles of prominent cartoonists. Ask students to choose an issue which inspires strong feelings in them and then create editorial cartoons which express their opinions.

— The masthead (sometimes called the staff box) appears in every issue of the editorial page. It lists staff members, owners, and the general editorial policy.

Have students review the masthead of their local community paper. What does it tell them? Why is it important that it appear on the editorial page?

— Ask students to consider why some papers print letters with a variety of opinions and others print only letters that appear to support the paper's editorial position. Have students examine several different papers to see if they can determi ne each paper's practice.

— Have students choose an editorial and analyze it for content, organization, and style. Ask them to write an editorial which takes a position opposed to this editorial and to include evidence for their position. They should outline the underlying principles or assumptions upon which their argument is built.

— Have students write an editorial on a controversial issue and deliver it to the class as an impassioned speech. After, have them discuss their performance and decide what aspects were fair comment and what might be considered prejudicial or unethical.

— Have students develop the arguments for only one side of an issue. Ask them to analyze the finished editorial for any unethical arguments. They might then write the editorial from another side of the issue. Again, they could analyze the finished editorial for unethical arguments.

— Letters to the editor are the readers' way of expressing their opinions. They are usually short, contain no libellous information, and include the names of the writers. Have students review examples from recent newspapers and note any similarities and differences.

— Have students develop a new look for the editorial page of a local or provincial newspaper.

— Columns are one person's opinions. They are identified by a consistent logo and by-line. Have students final examples of writers' columns (sports, entertainment, politics, interior design, etc.). Have them select a type of editorial column they would like to write, and then write their own column.

Feature Stories and Reviews

Features are not intended to deliver the news firsthand but to educate, illuminate, and entertain. They profile people who made the news; explain events that influenced the news; analyze what is happening locally, nationally, and internationally; examine trends in a changing society; and entertain.

Learning Objectives

Students will:

— listen to understand and learn

— compare, contrast, and evaluate texts

— recognize the importance for journalists of researching, interviewing, and reporting

— identify conventions of feature stories

— demonstrate fact gathering, research, and writing skills necessary for in-depth reporting

— conduct an interview skillfully

— write effective interview stories

— develop feature writing skills.

Activities

— Have students find several examples of feature stories

in a daily and weekly newspaper. Have them classify the features. Are they human interest stories, personality profiles, backgrounders, trend stories, or in-depth stories?

— Have students examine the lead and organization of several feature stories. How does the writer entice the reader into the story? Have students explain and give examples of various types of feature leads--narrative lead, contrast lead, question lead, quote lead, staccato lead, and direct address. Ask students to compare the feature stories with "hard news" stories.

— News and feature writers gather news and stories from investigative research. Preparation, research, accuracy, and questioning skills are all very important in investigative journalism. Have students develop and discuss possible interview questi ons, then conduct an interview and prepare a feature story profiling another student in the class.

— Have students tackle a sports issue. They might consider the role of sports in a scholastic setting, the costs of financing sports and athletes, sports injuries, or pressures placed on athletes. After interviewing players and coaches, they can write a feature article on their findings.

— Have students examine several reviews of the same film, video, or music. How are the reviews organized? How does each review open? How does it deal with content? What is the opinion of the reviewer? Ask students to view the video or film or listen to the music, and then write their own review.

— Some tabloids do not carry news. Instead they focus on feature stories which tend to be based on gossip and misinformation. This form of tabloid "news" has its roots in "yellow journalism", in which the facts are tinted to make them more interesting. Front pages of these tabloids use sensational headlines to convince readers to buy tabloids. Have students consider the form and layout of two tabloids. What size and style of print is used? What visuals and photography? What audiences do tabloids attract? Do these audiences believe what they read? Why do people read these papers? What is reflected in each story? In the paper as a whole? What types of stories are featured? How are their accounts similar or different?

— Have students read a story, narrative poem, or excerpt from a novel. Then, ask them to use the storyline to write as many different types of feature story leads as they can.

— One of the most important things a feature writer does is "set the scene". Using active verbs, colourful adjectives, and/or other techniques, the writer shows and tells what happened and captures the reader's attention. Ask students to identify the techniques used by several feature writers.

— Interviews with numerous credible sources are essential to feature stories. Have students compare the styles of two or more interviewers (e.g., Pamela Wallin on Newsworld and Larry King on Larry King Live). They might role play several interview situations to practise their skills. They could videotape their interviews and critique their performance.

— Have students prepare ten questions they would ask the Prime Minister, Premier, mayor, band councillor, or principal. Have students work in pairs to role play the interviews. They could videotape the interviews and then critique them. What worked and what did not? What was appropriate and what was not?

— Have students examine several sport stories in a newspaper or magazine. What evidence is there of the writer's knowledge of the game? What use was there of expressive language and descriptive words or phrases to create strong visual images of the action or issue? Have students write their own sports story about a coach or team in their community.

— Have students identify a lesser known sport that they feel needs more exposure and coverage. Have them write a feature explaining the key parts of the game--rules, scoring, terminology and generating interest in the sport.

— Have students assume the role of a freelance writer. Ask them to choose an event or person currently in the news and then write two stories--one for a traditional daily newspaper and one for a tabloid. They should decide what audience their stories will target in each paper and what specific ideas their stories will reflect. They should write the two stories about the same event or person, and then create their headlines and plan the visuals that will accompany each story.

11

Microsoft Solution for Intranets

The Microsoft Solution for Intranets includes integrated and tested software, prescriptive architectural guidance, and deployment services and support from Microsoft and experienced industry partners. Intranets are, by definition, holistic and necessitate an end-to-end infrastructure. Intranets are a complete infrastructure for productivity, collaboration, and knowledge management. This includes collaboration workspaces, general-purpose portals, portals designed for specific organizational functions, document management, enterprise-wide searches, ad hoc team sites, and real-time or on-demand access to digital media content.

The problem of effective information management for today's knowledge workers is all too painfully apparent. Even the simplest tasks seem to require massive effort or appear all but impossible. The only way to locate a document is to know where it was last saved. The only way to find a document someone else wrote is to request it from the author. The only way to keep track of the wide variety of online services a company makes available through its intranet is to maintain a very large "favorites" list in one's Web browser.

Every time a Web-based solution needs to be created, it has to be designed and developed from the ground up;

for example, in order to deliver dynamic SAP data into a portal for finance executives, an application would have to be specially written and repeatedly updated as application changes occur. When a project team is created, it is time-consuming or difficult to create shared facilities that the team can use to, for example, track tasks and share deliverables. If an executive or team leader needs to deliver an update to a broad, geographically dispersed audience, the standard ways to deliver such communication is via either e-mail or an in-person event. The use of digital media for corporate communications has grown in popularity, yet it has been a manual process that is difficult to administer and manage.

When documents and other content, such as streaming media, are organized into knowledge management solutions, users find such systems too cumbersome to actually use and resist using them. While individual approaches to information management remain significant, most content in the knowledge workplace is created collaboratively and accessed by distributed teams as a general-purpose resource, destined to be reused on an ongoing basis. Knowledge workers need improved and more efficient ways to share and use information within their organizations through intranets. Microsoft has designed its products and technologies to enable this practice. Microsoft SharePoint Portal Server 2001 is the flexible portal solution from Microsoft that allows companies to find, share, and publish information easily.

Microsoft SharePoint Team Services provides users with the ability to rapidly create and contribute to ad hoc team and project-focused Web sites. Microsoft Office XP provides a smarter way of working, simplifying the way individuals work, thus enabling easy collaboration and providing continual integration of additional services. Microsoft Windows Media Technologies provide the highest scalability and industry-leading audio and video quality, with tools designed specifically for an enterprise, making it easy for network administrators to centrally configure and manage the implementation of Windows Media within their organization. These products were developed as a direct result of customer feedback and research into effective information-sharing practices within business organizations. Each is a key element in the mix of technologies essential to intranets.

By combining the SharePoint and Windows Media technologies and Microsoft SQL Server 2000 into a single solution, customers can address the information-sharing challenges faced by both large and small groups within their enterprises. This solution gives users the ability to organize information, access that information, manage documents, and enable efficient collaboration-all in a familiar, browser-based and Microsoft Office-integrated environment.

Next generation intranets are designed to power the productivity of knowledge workers. They enable the knowledge workplace with Web-based collaborative team services, information management and discovery, and broadcast delivery of business communications to every desktop. Intranets provide a comprehensive solution for organizations, delivering effortless Web-based team collaboration, rapid access to business information, intuitive document management, and an end-to-end solution for broadcast communications to the desktop.

The Microsoft Solution for Intranets, is the most comprehensive intranet solution available today, integrating desktop productivity and collaboration with Microsoft Office XP; rich portal services with SharePoint Portal Server; team collaboration via SharePoint Team Services; management, production, and delivery of digital media communications; and data management with SQL Server-all running on the Windows operating system. The

Microsoft Solution for Intranets effectively enables document management, search, subscriptions, digital media broadcast, and ad hoc team-based collaboration. Its flexible portal architecture provides the facilities for constructing line-of-business (LOB) integrated portals, executive information systems, business analytical solutions, and many other applications that deliver unprecedented levels of knowledge worker efficiency, collaboration, and productivity.

WORKSPACES

A workspace is an online presence that provides a user interface, preferably one that is customizable and extensible; a storage facility for shared content; and a set of other application services either directly hosted within the workspace or to which the workspace provides a conduit. Workspaces are an important feature of intranets. Workspaces are also a social construct, a place for the work transactions that occur therein.

— Some workspaces will have very short life cycles, having been created for brief periods of time to serve the needs of particular projects. They will handle documents, to-do lists, calendar items, member lists, and so forth.

— Some workspaces will have similar requirements as project workspaces but with longer life cycles, although relevant only to relatively small teams.

— Other workspaces will address the needs of larger groups of people, often providing long-term storage of document content that spans a variety of usage patterns. Such sites will also address a variety of applications at the same time, consolidating a number of functions in a portal-based interface.

— Finally, a few workspaces will provide company-wide one-stop shopping to a well-defined set of services. Good examples of this include organization-wide content searching, organization-wide access to digital media (either broadcast in real time or made available for on-demand viewing by individual users), or a portal that makes human resources data viewable and (to an appropriate extent) editable by staff members.

The Solution's focus is to ensure that a comprehensive infrastructure exists for providing workspaces and organizing their content into an integrated network.

INFRASTRUCTURE

The infrastructure consists of four principal types of building blocks, organized into a manageable and coherent "hub-and-spoke" architecture. A central corporate portal provides one-stop searching of and linking to a wide variety of content, such as divisional portals, a broadcast media portal, formally managed team sites, ad hoc team sites, and external content. It serves as a common source of company-wide information, including announcements, news stories, training, calendar items, and a catalog of other Web sites. It also provides user subscriptions for a variety of new information, in which users receive notifications of the arrival of new documents pertaining to subjects in which they are interested.

Surrounding the central corporate portal in this hub-and-spoke arrangement is a set of divisional portals, each targeted to address the needs of up to 1000 users. Divisional portals provide document management services, search and subscription services to related team sites and external content, categorized views of content, and an application platform for integrating WebParts that provide access to a number of business applications. Single-purpose team sites are at the outer edge of this model, each targeted at 10 to 100 users, and designed for small groups or specific projects. They are linked to and indexed by the divisional portals around which they revolve and are also indexed by the corporate portal.

It is expected that half of these sites will be formally managed and half will be ad hoc sites. Formally managed sites are administered by designated staff. They can be created only by a defined set of such administrators and are indexed by both the corporate portal and their corresponding divisional portals. Such sites may even be the official presence for a given project or workgroup. Ad hoc sites encourage spontaneous collaboration and intrateam interaction. By default they can be created by any user when the need arises. They are not indexed by other portals, and there is no sense of the site being "published" for perusal by others. Work may well begin here before it is ready for a larger audience.

The Windows Media Broadcast component of the Microsoft Solution for Intranets provides a complete solution for managing, scheduling, producing, and delivering broadcast events, connecting employees to digital media broadcasts over the intranet. Enterprises today are using digital media primarily for corporate communications and training delivered via the intranet. As more demands are being placed on organizations to reduce costs and increase employee productivity, distributing communications to the desktop is imperative. The broadcast portal created using tne Windows Media Broadcast component occupies the same position in the hub-and-spoke hierarchy as a divisional portal and enables rapid implementation of a distributed audio/video broadcast environment for announcements, meetings, training, or other content to be delivered over the organization's intranet.

From the portal, organizations can configure and manage media distribution servers, optimize network bandwidth, schedule and manage live broadcast events, notify employees of events via their calendars, produce and deliver live events to employee desktops, and allow users to search for archived on-demand video presentations to view at their leisure. These capabilities have significant economic benefits over holding division or team meetings and help increase employee productivity and facilitate knowledge sharing within an organization. Access to and control over all this content is possible via a Web browser or directly through Microsoft Office XP. The tool most appropriate will depend on what the user is trying to accomplish at any given time.

Large organizations are typically composed of business divisions that are, in turn, composed of both large and small teams. These different organizational units share information in a variety of ways: within each team, between teams, across business divisions, and throughout the entire company. This solution offers companies a way to organize, manage, and share the wealth of information generated by these teams and divisions as well as by the larger corporation. Teams are formed to solve business problems. Team members need to be able to document, discuss, and share research in order to solve business problems. SharePoint Team Services host sites that provide a centralized and secure Web-based environment that includes document repositories, discussion groups, calendars, task lists, and site usage reporting.

Divisions are formed to unite teams within political or geographical business boundaries. Division members need to be able to track news and events relevant to their division. They also need to review content generated by other teams in their division that relates to their own team. The divisional portal provides a secure intranet site that includes division-wide news and announcements; events that affect the larger organization need to be communicated to all divisional teams and team members.

In addition, the divisional portal provides document management as well as search and subscription functionality. Users can then find the information they need and be alerted to the availability of new and relevant information.

Individual divisions may also need to provide applications to their users. A portal workspace, plus a catalog of reusable software components, makes it easy to assemble and deliver such focused solutions with high quality and low turnaround times. A corporate portal provides information at the enterprise level (news and announcements, navigation within and outside the organization) as well as access to aggregated information from the divisional and team levels (search and subscriptions). For any user in the organization, a variety of training, public information, or other material may be available either as a permanent collection of video on demand or as a series of scheduled broadcasts available to any desktop.

At all levels, content may be restricted to specific users or groups, enabling them to assume specific roles over specific sets of content. Given that all servers authenticate from a common directory or set of domains, access control is preserved and respected at all levels of the workspace hierarchy.

The key to delivering the functionality and performance outlined by this solution is the deployment of servers to deliver specialized functions. The corporate portal is actually a single server running SharePoint Portal Server 2001 with Service Pack 1. This server hosts the portal homepage and all the prescribed WebParts, corporate-wide search, and subscriptions. It does not directly index any content sources but instead receives regular index updates from the content index server. It provides no document management services of its own, although some of its WebParts provide direct links to the divisional portals and team sites hosted on other servers.

The content index server indexes all content across the various intranet and Internet servers and forwards its results to the corporate portal, which is a physical server running SharePoint Portal Server 2001 with Microsoft Service Pack 1. It can be configured to crawl file shares, Web sites, Microsoft Exchange public folders, Lotus Notes databases, and SharePoint Team Services sites. While it is kept quite busy, all of its activity occurs in the background relative to the activities of other servers.

A divisional portal is a physical server running SharePoint Portal Server 2001 with Service Pack 1. It hosts the dashboard-based portals used by division members, processes search requests for local content as well as content in federated team site servers, and provides document management services. This server is configured to support 1000 users performing a variety of tasks. Other WebParts and sub-dashboards may be customized after deployment to provide division-specific application functionality. The team sites for a division are delivered using a physical server running SharePoint Team Services and SQL Server 2000. This server stores the content for all team sites. It is configured to support up to 1000 users spread across 100 team sites.

The broadcast portal is a single server running SharePoint Portal Server 2001 together with a custom Active Server Pages application running under Microsoft Internet Information Server 5.0. It fits into the overall intranet architecture by having its content indexed by the content index server for use by the corporate portal. The corporate portal also provides links that carry users directly to the portal. The broadcast portal server hosts an application that provides management, organization, and scheduling functionality for digital media. Broadcast events can be searched or browsed by users, and selecting a media event results in a connection to the most appropriate distribution server.

The portal server can also send appointment items to Exchange Server 2000 calendars that automatically handle connection to a live multicast when it takes place. Windows Media Servers are dedicated Microsoft Windows 2000 Servers and provide the actual storage and streaming distribution of digital media content. The fact that Windows Media Services is built into a Windows 2000 Server means that you can take advantage of the operating system's reliability, scalability, performance, and cost-effectiveness. The Digital Media Workstation provides the production console where media content is captured and encoded into digital formats and placed on Windows Media Servers. It works in conjunction with the Broadcast Media Portal to provide both production facilities and ease of logistics when making them available to users.

No intranet solution will be successful if users avoid it. No interface is ideal for all tasks. The Microsoft Solution for Intranets encourages using the right tool for the right task at the right time. Two primary interfaces exist for accessing portal and team site content:

(1) Microsoft Internet Explorer for browsing, search, and Web portal application access, which can be used to handle document management facilities; or

(2) Microsoft Office XP to provide the optimal interface for document navigation, management, authoring, and administration of content maintained on the divisional portals. Office XP also provides several facilities that leverage the corporate portal's search facility from within Microsoft Word, Excel, and PowerPoint.

While many if not most document management tasks can be performed exclusively within a Web browser environment, using SharePoint Portal Server and Office XP together makes documents more discoverable; the business process around finding, sharing, and publishing documents thus becomes more mainstream. Support for SharePoint Portal Server ships with every copy of Office XP. Consider the following:

— With Microsoft Office XP's client for SharePoint Portal Server 2001, the workspace's content is as easy to navigate as the folders on a user's local disk drives. All extended document information can be seen via task panes, used as column headings in folder views, and edited via property pages.

— Within Microsoft Word, Excel, and PowerPoint, document check-in/check-out, publishing, categorization, versioning, and profiling become as easy as opening or saving a file. Document management functions appear on menus and toolbars, and dialog boxes that prompt for categories and profile information appear from within these native applications.

Consider the alternative, which would involve accessing the portal with a browser, downloading the document to one's local disk drive, editing it with one's word processor, saving it, returning to the portal from one's browser, uploading the new version of the document, providing additional profile and category information, and then saving the new information with the uploaded file. The difference in effort and time is more than a matter of convenience-it is a matter of productivity.

Office XP also allows for the unified searching of documents from within its File menus, allowing a single search to examine local drives, Microsoft Outlook message content, and anything a SharePoint Portal Server can index . This is done from within the native application; no separate trip to a Web browser is necessary. Smart tags, a technology in Office XP that allows for custom, context-specific code to appear on demand when specific text is present, are available to directly link to SharePoint Portal Server categories and searches from within Office XP documents. Moreover, Office XP isn't just a tool for using the content of a SharePoint Portal Server workspace; it can help create the portal as well.

Documents created in Office XP applications and saved using the "Save as WebPart" functionality can, in turn, become part of a portal. This allows users to contribute to a divisional portal's home dashboard and even create entire personal dashboards composed exclusively of Office XP-authored content. A set of spreadsheets, for example, can be saved as WebParts to create a business intelligence application hosted within a divisional portal-with very little time and effort necessary to go from a document to a WebPart that can be used and reused by a variety of portals.

The Microsoft Solution for Intranets reflects a practice-based, open-ended architecture for providing collaborative workspaces and other knowledge management services. It was designed to provide specific hardware and configuration specifications in order to yield a well-tested, well-measured level of well-defined performance. Each type of server is provided with a specific usage scenario that translates into a given server load. This prescriptive architecture delivers performance numbers that meet the demands of these usage scenarios.

The divisional workspace's portal is intended to host the homepage and the central repository of information for large teams within a business division. Teams within the division can store and manage documents within the workspace, meaning that updates to the site take place frequently and by many users. Most users probably visit this portal during any given day. The typical activity under which this scenario has been tested involves multiple visits to the homepage, browsing the document library, browsing category listings, searches, opening documents, saving documents, and performing check-ins/check-outs. Team sites help project groups and ad hoc teams share information; the architecture supports up to 100 team sites, with 10 users per site, on relatively modest hardware. The scenario expects most of a site's users to use the site during a given day and further assumes several visits to the homepage, several document postings and retrievals, and several list perusals and contributions.

The broadcast portal, like the corporate portal, can be visited at any time by anyone in the organization, but the total number of users accessing the portal at any one time usually falls short of the company's total population. The exception to this is, of course, a company-wide real-time broadcast. In addition, client time spent at the portal is usually a fraction of the time spent connected directly to the Windows Media Server-hosted content the portal makes available. For real-time broadcasts, scaling to 15,000 users is quite possible, particularly when multicasting is leveraged aggressively. For on-demand content, redundant copies of media placed on multiple servers allows for both load balancing and minimizing wide-area bandwidth.

12

Elements of Data Analysis

Strategies for data analysis vary depending on whether you are dealing with continuous data or categorical data. Continuous data places, for practical purposes, no limits on values, and so it preserves fine differences, for example, the difference between an annual income of $32,456 and one of $32,460. Categorical data sort things into bins. Public opinion surveys, for example, usually use only four or five categories to represent all possible incomes. Categorical data are often more convenient to handle, but the convenience comes at the cost of losing some of the information. We will assume continuous data, most commonly found in government reports, such as the census, and in economic statistics.

Figuring a Rate

One way to build a comparison into a number is to convert it into a rate. That procedure automatically provides a comparison against some easily recognized baseline. The number of deaths from AIDS for each nation is not as meaningful as the number of deaths per 100,000 population. By converting the raw number to a rate, you assess the impact on the population, and you provide a way to compare relative impact from one country to another regardless of differences in population size. The most commonly used rate is the rate per hundred (per centum, in Latin) or percent. A percent is the decimal equivalent of a fraction, but with the decimal point moved two places to the right. Thus:

$$1/2 = .5 = 50\%$$

The first rule of percentages is this:

> No percentage makes sense unless you know its base.

The way to figure a percent without losing track of the base is to get the fraction first. If 11 members of the 42-man 1986 football squad graduated in four years, the squad's four-year graduation rate is 11/42. The 11 in the fraction is the number who graduated, and the 42 is the base to which the number who graduated is being compared. The base is the bottom of the fraction. When you have the base firmly in mind, you can convert the fraction to a decimal by division. Don't forget the two-place move of the decimal point implied in the concept of percent:

.5 = five-tenths = .50 = 50 hundredths

Fifty percent is another and easier way of saying 50 hundredths. If we left the decimal where it was and said .50 hundredths or .5 percent we would have more than a redundancy, we would have an entirely different number (one-half of one percent). Sometimes you will see in print expressions like .50 percent where the writer really means 50 percent. The decimal point was evidently thrown in just for emphasis. So here is another rule of life:

> Decimal points are for meaning, not for emphasis.

Sometimes the rate you are describing will be so small that it needs to be expressed in fractions of a percentage point. In that case, consider expressing it as a rate per 1,000 or rate per 100,000, whatever leaves you with whole numbers to compare. That will reduce the chance of typographical error as well as of misunderstanding.

Percent Difference

Percent difference means just what it says: the difference between two values taken as a percentage of whichever value you are using as the base. If you want the percent change from Time 1 to Time 2, then the Time 1 value is the base. So first obtain the absolute value of the difference. Subtract 2668.26 from 2759.84, and you find that the Dow dropped 190.58 points. Now you can set up the fraction. (Be sure you use the right base.) The percent decline is:

$$\frac{190.58}{2759.84} = .0690547 = 6.91\%$$

Notice that to get from the decimal to the percent we moved the decimal two places to the right and added a percent sign. We also rounded to two decimal places, which is probably more precision than we need, but we bow to Wall Street Journal style. Notice also that rounding is not the same as truncating. If we truncated, we would come out with 6.90 percent. But since the dropped value is more than half, we round up to 6.91. To evaluate the dropped digits put an imaginary decimal in front of them. So the market fell 6.91 percent on Friday the 13th.

Now try this question: What percent gain does the market have to make from Friday's close to regain its status at Thursday's close? Perhaps you think that since it went down 6.91 percent, it has to go up 6.91 percent to get back to where it was. Not so! It has to go back up the same 190.58 in absolute points, but in framing this question we switched the percentage base. The base is now Friday's close, and so:

$$\frac{190.58}{2759.84} = .0741603 = 7.42\%$$

To recover from its 6.91 percent loss, the market had to gain 7.42 percent. After that Friday-the-13th drop, a television newscaster refer to it as the second biggest drop in history. That was true in absolute points, but in percentage terms it was only the 12th. Here is the record, taken from the Wall Street Journal:1

Date	Close	Point Change	Percent Change
Oct. 19, 1987	1738.74	-508.00	-22.61
Oct. 28, 1929	260.64	-38.33	-12.82
Oct. 29, 1929	230.07	-30.57	-11.73
Nov. 6, 1929	232.13	-25.55	-9.92
Aug. 12, 1932	63.11	-5.79	-8.40
Oct. 26, 1987	1793.93	-156.83	-8.04
July 21, 1933	88.71	-7.55	-7.84
Oct. 18, 1937	125.73	-10.57	7.75
Oct. 5, 1932	66.07	-5.09	-7.15
Sept. 24, 1931	107.79	-8.20	-7.07
July 20, 1933	96.26	-7.32	-7.07
Oct. 13, 1989	2569.26	-190.58	-6.91

It is obvious that the relevant comparison is percentage change, not absolute change. A 100-point drop in the early depression years would have wiped out the entire market. Today, it jolts it, but it is hardly anything like a disaster. And yet news media tend to focus on the absolute change when making historical comparisons, as though there were no difference in a Dow of 200 and one of 2,000. In 1986, when the sharp changes induced by program trading began to rock the market, stories of "record declines" were routine.

Television was the worst offender, but even wire service writers were not always careful to specify that they were talking about point declines and not percent declines when they drew comparisons. For example, an Associated Press lead on November 18, 1986, said, "Worries about Wall Street's insider trading scandal sent stock prices reeling Tuesday, and the Dow Jones industrial average recorded its fourth biggest drop ever." Not until the eighth paragraph did the writer confess that, in relative terms, the drop was only 2.3 percent, which is of little historical significance and nowhere near the fourth biggest ever, which at that time was the 8.4 percent drop in 1932.

That pattern, hyping the story by focusing on the point decline and then backpedaling to tell what really happened in percentage terms, was the pattern for the AP and other print media throughout 1986 and 1987 until a really historic crash occurred on October 19, 1987. When the market really did experience a record decline — 22.61 percent — there was no way to make the lead any stronger than the ones that had hyped the record point declines throughout 1986 and 1987. After that, the reporting got more realistic, but many writers still prefer to give priority to the less important point comparison simply because it yields a bigger number. That it is a misleading number does not seem to matter to them.

The reasons for the Dow being so much higher now than it was in the 1930s are straightforward. The economy has grown and companies are worth more. Part of the growth is real and part is inflation. These are secular trends, meaning that they affect just about everything in society. If you are going to make comparisons across time, you have to filter out that secular effect in order to see what is going on specifically with the phenomenon you are investigating. In other words, you need to detrend the numbers, to use a term favored by Cook and Campbell. Expressing change in percentage terms is one way to detrend, but it is not the only way. Adjusting the Dow Jones for inflation would be another.

Financial analysts and accountants do not routinely do that, but if they did, the effect on the Dow Jones Industrial Average would be eye-opening. Its long-term growth, though still real, would not be nearly as impressive.

Times More v. Times As

Before leaving the problem of figuring a percent difference, we need to consider the case of a percent difference greater than 100. The Dow Jones industrials closed at 2759.84 on October 12, 1989, and at 230.07 on October 29, 1929. How much did the Dow increase over that sixty-year period? The same formula applies. To get the percent difference, use subtraction to get the absolute difference and divide by the value for the base year. Thus:

$$\% \text{ difference} = (2759.84 - 230.07)/230.07$$

Some people use the rule "Divide the little number by the big number." That's the wrong rule. It only works if the percentage difference is going to be less than 100. In our sixty-year comparison, where the value for the base year is smaller than the value for the comparison year, the Dow industrial average increased by 1100 percent. What does an increase of 1100 percent mean? Another way to express it would be to say that the industrial average was "11 times greater" in October 1989 than in October 1929.

Times greater compares the base value to the difference (the amount "greater"). And "times as great" compares the base value to the new value. The 1989 number, 2759.84 is 12 times the 1929 figure of 230.07. It is only 11 times the difference. That is clear enough once you think about it. Unfortunately, many news writers do not think about it and use "times greater" and "times as" interchangeably as if they meant the same thing. They don't!Consider this example from the Atlanta Journal-Constitution:

> Washington —An assault gun is 20 times more likely to be used in crime than a conventional firearm, according to a study by the Atlanta Journal-Constitution Washington Bureau. While assault guns account for 1 million —or 0.5 percent — of the 200 million privately owned firearms in the United States, they were used in one of every 10 crimes that resulted in a firearms trace last year, the study shows.

The comparison of the incidence of assault guns with the expected incidence is perfectly reasonable. But 10 percent is 19 times greater than half a percent, not 20 times greater. It is, however, 20 times as great, which is probably what the writers meant to say.

Adjusting for Inflation

When dollar amounts are compared across time, it is usually a good idea to detrend the figures by taking out the effect of inflation. One barrier to doing this is the lack of a good statistical indicator of inflation. The most common one is the Consumer Price Index of the Bureau of Labor Statistics. It was created during World War I when runaway prices, especially in ship-building centers, made it necessary to make frequent cost-of-living adjustments in wages. The CPI shows the relative value of a dollar's purchasing power from year to year. It does this by checking the price of a "market basket" of goods and services that is held relatively constant over time.

The market basket includes food, clothing, shelter, fuels, transportation, medical services, and other things that people buy for daily living. The problem comes in trying to define a market basket that means the same thing in 1990 as in, say, 1952. Some goods and services that are relevant and considered necessary in 1990 did not exist in

1952: antipollution equipment for cars, for example. The Bureau tries to solve this problem by redefining the market basket from time to time to keep it abreast of changing life-styles and technology. Even so, it is not possible to create one market basket that applies equally to all groups.

For example, retirees who own their homes are not affected by changes in rental or home values. For home-owning federal government retirees, whose pensions are indexed to the CPI, the indexing creates a windfall. Their incomes automatically go up more than their own normal living costs. Such indexing is, of course, a form of detrending, squeezing out the secular trend of inflation so that you can see the real meaning. Doing it only approximately is better than not doing it at all, as the millions of retirees living on non-indexed private pensions, whose real value shrinks year by year, will agree. And yet accountants don't like to index or detrend because of the element of uncertainty that it introduces into their work.

Corporate balance sheets seldom show the effect of inflation. Press releases boasting of record profits sometimes show profits that would be below historic levels if constant dollar comparisons were made. Labor leaders have made the same idle boasts, taking credit for gains that are really losses when they are detrended for inflation. The procedure for detrending for inflation is simple. When you compare dollar amounts across time, express them in the constant dollars of one of your comparison years. When one of the years being compared is the current year, the usual practice is to convert the older amounts into their current equivalents or constant dollars. But it can just as easily be done the other way.

Here is an example close to home. David H. Weaver and G. Cleveland Wilhoit reported in 1986 that the median income of journalists had increased from $11,133 in 1970 to $19,000 in 1981. That was bad news for journalists, they pointed out, because the intervening period was one of raging inflation, and the journalists actually lost about \$7,000 a year in purchasing power.6 To verify their calculation, you need the CPI for 1970 and for 1981. According to the Statistical Abstract of the United States, published annually by the U.S. Government Printing Office, it was 38.8 and 90.9, respectively (the index uses the prices for the 1982-1984 period as a base of 100). Then convert the median journalistic income for 1970 into constant 1981 dollars. Use the formula for fraction equivalents that you learned in high school:

$$\frac{38.8}{11{,}133} = \frac{90.9}{X}$$

Perhaps you are more comfortable with an English sentence than an equation: 38.8 is to \$11,133 as 90.9 is to the unknown quantity (1970's income expressed in 1981 constant dollars). Following the cross-multiplication rule from your high school algebra, you find that:

$$38.8 * X = 11{,}133 * 90.9$$

Dividing each side of the equation by 38.8 yields:

$$X = (11{,}133 * 90.9)/38.8$$

Punch it into your calculator, and 1970's \$11,133 turns out to be equal to \$26,082.21 in constant 1981 dollars. So the wages of journalism actually fell by 27 percent over that period. How come? Two things happened. The performance of two young Washington Post reporters in the Watergate scandal motivated many young people to become journalists. In the same time, barriers to women in the profession were lowered. Both events greatly increased the pool of available workers in journalism. This windfall of idealistic, motivated youth gave the owners of the media a wonderful choice. (1) raise the standards of journalism by tapping the best of the enlarged pool and welcoming the best and the brightest into journalism. (2) choose the next generation of journalists by selecting those who would work for the least amount of money and carry the savings to the bottom line.

Adjusting Population Growth

Trends make news, either because they have been going on quietly and not many have noticed or because of a sudden interruption in a trend. To focus on the newsworthy trend, you have to separate it from all the parallel trends in the background. Population growth is one secular trend that, like inflation, can make other trends be more or less than they seem. The American Newspaper Publishers Association every year issues a booklet of statistical trends in the news business. It shows that newspaper circulation grows a little bit every year in the United States. That sounds like good news for newspapers, but it is not, because the population and the number of households is growing a lot faster. Circulation penetration, defined as circulation divided by households, has been dropping steadily over the years, and that is the number ANPA really cares about, even though it does not publish it in its booklet.

It is a number that is easy to understand at the intuitive level. When penetration was at 100 percent in a given market, one newspaper was sold for every household. When it was above 100 percent, more newspapers were sold than there were households — common in the 1950s. Today the number is much smaller and still falling, with some metropolitan newspapers experiencing household penetration of less than 50 percent. Expressing newspaper circulation as a ratio to households (because home-delivered circulation is sold to households rather than to individuals) makes the real trend easier to see (Figure 1).

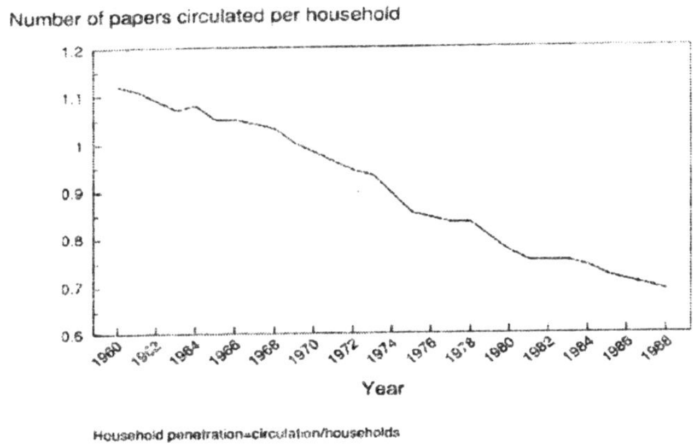

Figure 1. Newspaper household penetration 1960-1988

For an extreme example of population growth as a confounding factor. A scatterplot shows each data point in a two-dimensional space. In this case, the vertical dimension represents church membership (higher is more) and the horizontal dimension represents liquor sales (rightward is more). Each data point is a year, represented by a dot placed according to the church membership and the liquor sales for that year.

Just by looking at the scatterplot (Figure 2), you can see that the greater the church membership, the greater the liquor sales. In fact, the correlation is almost perfect. The fun part is producing theories to explain it — for example, church-going relieves people of guilt, and so they feel free to drink; or drinking makes people feel guilty, and so they go to church. Of course, both are explained by population growth, and when we detrend the numbers by expressing them as ratios to population, the association disappears.

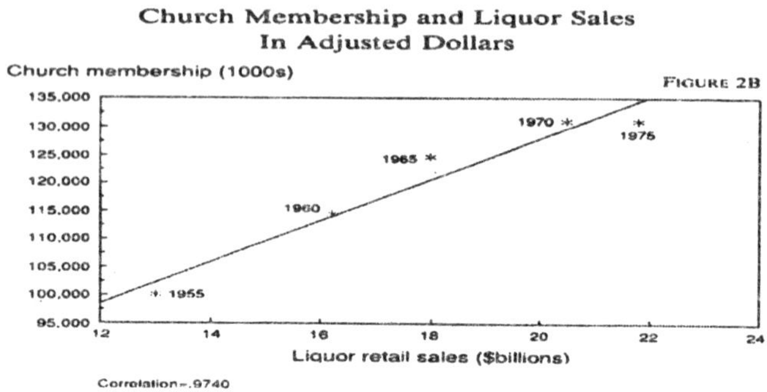

Figure 2.

Where do you get population numbers to use in detrending? The U.S. census is collected only every ten years, but lots of organizations produce interim estimates for the intervening years. Standard Rate and Data Service produces media audience studies and population estimates, and its reports are available in larger libraries and in the marketing departments of media organizations. The Audit Bureau of Circulations has county-level household estimates year by year. Most newspapers and many journalism schools are ABC members and have access to its data, both in print form and on PC diskette.

Curve Fitting

Sometimes interesting trends are confused by a variety of factors, including random error. Survey research based on sample data is subject to random error, particularly when small subgroups are examined. One way to get a clearer picture of a trend is to try to fit it to a smooth line. A straight-line fit works for many kinds of trend data. You can use your calculator or a statistical program, such as SPSS (Statistical Package for the Social Sciences), to do a regression and scatterplot with time as the independent or X variable. The correlation coefficient will tell you how well your data fit the straight-line model. If it is a good fit, you can even try to predict the future by drawing in the best-fitting straight line and extending it with a straightedge. Such a linear projection tells you what will happen if present trends continue unchanged — which, of course, they may not do.

Nature, unfortunately, is not fond of straight lines. Not to worry. You can use the same regression program to fit a curved line. First, examine the scatterplot and use your imagination to see what kind of a line might fit. If it is a simple curve, one that does not twist in a new direction at some point along its length, you can sometimes straighten it out by reexpressing one of the variables in terms of some nonlinear function. If your curve is hollow upward, to use Tukey's term, try an expression to the right of Y. If it is hollow downward, move to the left. Do the reverse to reexpress the independent or X variable. Check your scatterplot each time you try one of these conversions to see if the curve is straightening out. If it works, and if you try to predict the future with the straightedge technique, remember that it is a prediction based on a transformation of Y or X, and you will have to convert it back before your prediction will make any sense.

SMOOTHING

The most interesting trends are often those that twist and turn the most exotically. Tukey has a procedure for dealing with such convoluted data that he calls "smoothing." The theory behind smoothing is that measurement error is itself a secular trend and can be taken out by using each point as a check on the neighboring points. A rolling average is a fairly familiar method of smoothing. If you have monthly data that need smoothing, express January as the mean of December, January, and February. Then for February, use the mean of January, February, and March. Tukey's recommendation is to use rolling medians of three rather than means. Here's how to do that: compare each data point with those on either side and then replace it with the middle one of the three.

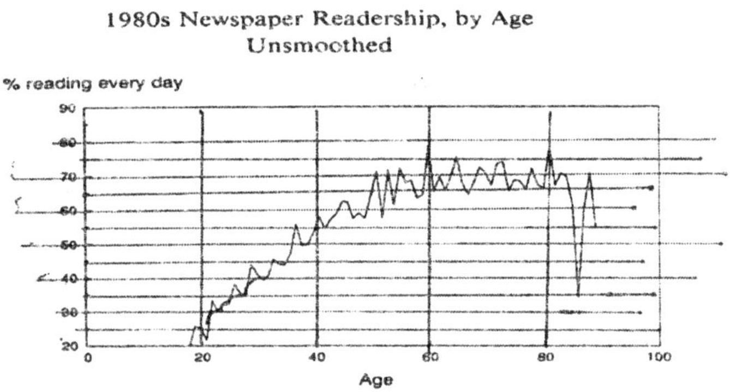

Figure 3.

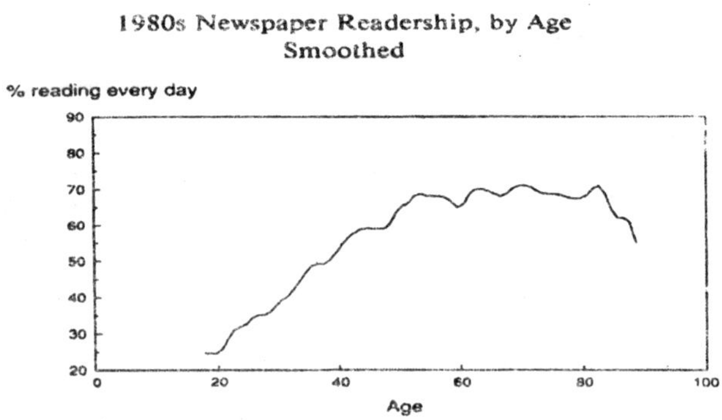

Figure 4.

For example, in the series 324, the two would be changed to a three because three is the median of the set. That way, wildly out-of-range points will be buried. That's good, says Tukey, because those oddball points catch the eye and make it difficult to see what is really going on. "The value of smoothing," he says, ". . . is the clearer view of the general, once it is unencumbered by detail." In other words, it is exactly what a journalist needs. And if one smooth of running medians of three leaves some jagged places, Tukey recommends doing it again — and again — until smoothing no longer changes things. Figure 3 shows a plot of daily newspaper readership by exact age. Its purpose is to see how readership changes according to life stage. The smoothed version, fig. 4, makes this clearer.

Index Numbers

Another way to achieve clarity for analysis and communication is to use index numbers. The CPI is a good example of an index number. With 1982-1984 set at 100, and September 1989 at 125, you know that prices rose 25 percent from the base period. Newspaper advertising sales people sometimes use index numbers to compare a newspaper's audience with its market. If 35 percent of the adults in the market have college degrees and 47 percent of the readers have college degrees, the index is 134. This is another way of saying that the rate of college graduation is 34 percent higher among readers than in the market as a whole. By applying this indexing to a variety of competing media, the ad salesman can make the case that his paper's readership is more upscale and has more buying power than the raw circulation numbers would indicate.

Seasonal Adjustment

Another form of detrending is seasonal adjustment. When the Bureau of Labor Statistics issues its monthly unemployment figures, it gives us numbers that can be directly compared from one month to the next so that we can see at a glance whether things are getting better or worse. But unemployment is seasonal. School openings and closings and climate conditions can affect the number of people looking for work at different times of the year. To assess the health of the economy, we are interested in the month-to-month changes that cannot be ascribed to the seasonal variation.

The BLS statisticians perform this detrending by looking at past seasonal changes and assuming that the current year will not be very different. Then they subtract the portion attributable to the change in season and report the rest. There is some risk in this, of course, because the seasonal variations are not uniform from year to year. But it is better than not doing it at all. If the White House puts out unemployment numbers in the fall of an election year that show a dramatic drop in unemployment, careful reporters will check to be sure that the seasonal adjustment has not been omitted. If it has, the decline can be merely the result of much of the teenage labor force going back to school.

Regression Residuals

A statistical technique for detrending comes in handy when you need to control for some overpowering continuous variable that conceals most of what you are interested in. Andrew Brack was studying the editorial quality of newspapers in North Carolina, but he was handicapped by the fact that circulation size explains most of the variance. Bigger papers have more resources, and so they give their readers more for their money. Brack nevertheless assembled a sample of large and small papers, measured them on a number of indicators of editorial quality, combined the indicators into an index and plotted them on a chart.

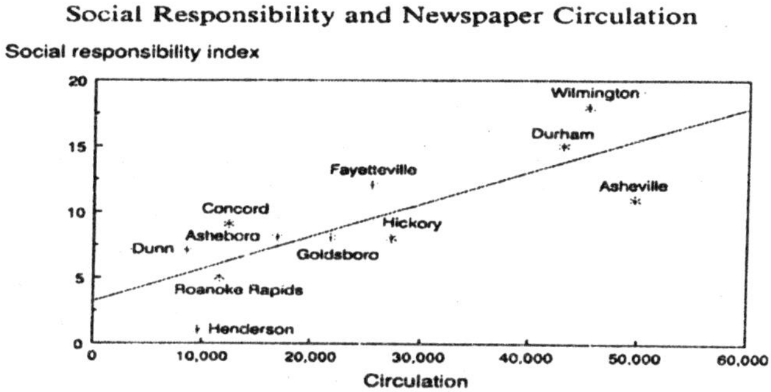

Figure 5.

Using the general linear model (GLM) to plot the best-fitting straight line for describing the effect of circulation on quality, Brack then turned his attention to the deviations from that line. Some papers were much higher in quality than would be predicted by their circulation size, and others were much lower. By measuring those deviations from what circulation would predict, he obtained a detrended measure of quality that eliminated the effect of circulation size. The technical term for this technique is residual analysis, because it looks at the residual variance, or the variance that is left over after circulation size explains what it can.

Standardized Scores

Another way to put apples and oranges on a comparable basis is to use standardized or z-scores, which reexpress each measurement in terms of how much it deviates from a group average. It is useful if you have a number of measures to combine into an index but can't use simple addition because each measure is on a different scale. A z-score is a measure of relative peculiarity

13

Free Media

Independence of the media is a very complex concept. In general terms, it focuses onthe notion that journalists should be free from any form of interference in the pursuit andpractice of their profession. In reality, the owners of the media intervene daily in theoperations of the journalists in their employment. In many countries, the government itself isthe largest media owner (often of the leading television and radio stations)—a situation which undermines the very concept of ensuring the genuine independence of the media from theinfluences of the state. The rights of journalists in state-owned media enterprises and the degree of freedom theyenjoy is sometimes, but not always, stipulated and guaranteed in law.

The lack of legislation and regulation in this context is a direct threat to the independence of the media. In the UK, for example, where the BBC is widely seen as operating at arms-length from the governmentand enjoying more independence than many state-owned media outlets in other countries, the Thatcher government explicitly banned the BBC, along with the private media, from broadcastingdirect interviews with leaders of the Irish Republican Army. There is obviously validityto the argument that "a financially dependent media cannot be truly free". Efforts should be undertaken to strengthen the independence of the media through theprivatisation of existing state-owned or controlled media.

The systems must be developed which ensure a diversity of media ownership, so that competitionwithin the media stimulates a wide range of perspectives on public policy issues and acts as acheck on the political power of media magnates. A free, privately-owned media is only possible when there is meaningful competition in the media marketplace. Rivalry in the market makes the corrupt newspaper owner fearful of exposure, just as it serves as a deterrent to the corrupt public office holder. In late 1994, for example, a book publishing company owned by News Corporation (a global enterprise headed byRupert Murdoch) offered US$4. 5 million in advance payments to Congressman Newt Gingrich, then Speaker of the U. S. House of Representatives, for two books. Very swiftly, many mediaoutlets reported the offer and some suggested the possibility that Mr. Murdoch, who had majorissues before Washington governmental bodies regarding his television interests, had offereda bribe to the new Republican Party leader. Reporting by the media forced the cancellation ofthe book deal.

However, many countries do not have the same abundance of media owners; rivalry is far less intense and, at times, media "cartels" can be formed to suit the political interestsof the day. In some cases, one family "rules" the media in a country. Such an overwhelminglydominant position means that media magnates need not fear exposure by rivals, and in an age of electronic media, their political power can enable them greatly to influencethe outcomes of elections. Furthermore, many developing countries have very little advertising money available to supportthe media. As a consequence, the media in these countries is desperately underfundedand, at times, dependent. On the one hand, large advertisers (of which the government is usuallyamong the most prominent) exert enormous control, and on the other, political and businessentities have a wide scope to bribe reporters (who tend to be very poorly paid) to writestories that serve their political and business interests. In these types of situations, the media frequently fails to perform its watch dog role.

The media privatisation process, just like the broader issues of media ownership, must therefore be carefully considered within its social and economic context. Monopolies in the media area are potentially even more dangerous than aremonopolies in other areas of economic life. In numerous instances, governments assert that their democratic institutions are still fragileand their free media inexperienced, and argue that there is merit in continued governmentalownership. This is often the case, but in such circumstances, the state-owned media should notenjoy a monopoly. In countries where governments insist on retaining some measure of control, safeguards or an independent regulator should be in place to stand between the Governmentand the rights of a free media.

Guarantor of a Free Media

Censorship of the media takes many forms and raises its head in almost all countries. Few have legal systems which guarantee absolute freedom of the media. Amendment 1 to the Constitutionof the United States, as tested before the U. S. Supreme Court, comes as close to guaranteeinga society free of censorship as any particular legislative act. The Constitution of Malawi is unique in this regard as it enshrines the concept of the freedom of the media not once, buttwice, and in the following terms:

— Every person shall have the right to freedom of expression and,

— The press shall have the right to report and publish freely, within Malawi and abroad, and to be accorded the fullest possible facilities for access to public information.

Laws declaring "freedom of expression" require support and enforcement from the courts. An independent judiciary is the handmaiden of a free media. Without an independent judiciary, media freedom is likely to be illusory. A prerequisite for building a free media, therefore, is alegal system that is independent of political influence and has a firm constitutional jurisprudencesupporting the concept of a free media. Such jurisprudence can draw strength from Article19 of the International Covenant on Civil and Political Rights, which states: Everyone shall have the right to freedom of opinion and expression; this right shallinclude freedom to seek, receive and impart information and ideas of all kinds, regardless of frontiers, either orally, in writing or in print, in the form of art, orthrough any other media of his choice.

Restrictions on these widely-accepted rights relate to the rights or reputations of private individuals and to matters of national security. Although many journalists would accept that suchrestrictions are reasonable, they would almost all agree that they must be narrowly interpreted. The legal and regulatory frameworks should not, for example, provide restrictions on themedia that may prevent them from publishing matters simply because these could damage thepublic reputation of public office holders. To do so would, in fact, undermine freedom of expression. A decision by the European Court on Human Rights held that the politician "inevitably and knowingly lays himself open to close scrutiny of his every word and deed byboth journalists and the public at large, and he must display a greater degree of tolerance".

However, in many young and fragile democracies the media's experience is limited and thetemptation to be less responsible is significant. Laws which, in essence, provide full scope forthe media to be irresponsible, may actually damage the growth of these emerging democracies. In this regard, there may be merit in the establishment of Press Councils. Although PressCouncils have not generally been very successful, they can be constructed so as to provide anopen forum for complaints against the media by the public, to chastise the media when it isirresponsible, and through these means, influence (to a degree) its behaviour.

Press Councils need to be independent and directed by people widely respected for their non-partisanstanding and their integrity. These bodies should not have powers of legal sanction, which could enable them to become powerful censors. Rather, they should have the prestigeand integrity that give their reports strong moral force. A useful requirement is for the subjectof a complaint to be required to publish, in full and unedited, the findings of the Press Councilwhere a complaint against it has been upheld.

A very fine line exists between responsible and irresponsible journalism. As such, time andplace are important factors that should influence judgements. Indeed, the moral force of aPress Council is a better way to secure a responsible media, than to provide governments andcourts with wide-ranging powers to curb it. Assertions of media irresponsibility often lead to calls for laws and systems that guarantee only a "reasonably" free media. Experience showsthat the term "reasonably" is highly subjective, and that acceptance of it in this context canbe the first step down a slippery slope towards diverse forms of censorship.

The "reasonably" approach often comes to the fore in matters relating to national security. The Official Secrets Act in the U. K. , and similar legislation in other countries, can provide anumbrella for all manner of secret activity by a government. For example, President Nixonattempted, in the early 1970s, to withhold tapes of conversations in the White House from thecourts and the Congress on the grounds of national security. Following the eventual publicationof the tapes, however, few argued that their publication had been damaging to thenation's security.

Government officials, conditioned over many decades to label items "confidential, " or "secret, "or "top secret, " build a strong prejudice against public disclosure of information, and frequently seek to prevent disclosure through claims of national security. It is important, whenestablishing best practices, that the independent judiciary be objective in assessing theseclaims. It should take the view that all government documentation should be in the public domain and open to public scrutiny, unless there is a forceful and compelling argument, presented by the government, for maintaining secrecy. Secrecy is more often justifiable on thegrounds of the legitimate protection of personal privacy or the maintenance of commercialconfidentiality, than it is on the (relatively rare) grounds of protecting national security.

The most effective system for guaranteeing freedom of the media is one where the media itselfis empowered to make careful judgements on its own. To provide publishers and journalists with freedom is also to burden them with difficult decisions regarding public responsibility. In the1960s, The New York Times received several thousand pages of documents from a source withinthe U. S. Department of Defence. These documents, which dealt with the war in Vietnam, becameknown as the "Pentagon Papers". The editors of the New York Times, after assuring themselvesof the authenticity of the documents, agonised for days over whether or not it was responsibleto publish them. They weighed considerations of national security against the public's right toknow. They decided to publish. Their decision was not taken lightly and it emerged that manyindividuals of experience, in public affairs, the law and the media had different perspectives onthe issue. None could claim a monopoly of wisdom, and none claimed that the judgements ofjournalists were necessarily inferior to those of experts from other professions.

The decision to publish the "Pentagon Papers" was carefully reviewed by the courts, whichconcluded that the freedom of the media, as expressed in the First Amendment to the U. S. Constitution, was of greater significance in this instance than national security claims made bythe U. S. Government. Consistent judgments of this kind by an independent court system canserve, over time, to build a tradition of media freedom. Such a tradition can be fortified by"sunshine laws", such as the U. S. Freedom of Information Act 1966, which enable every citizento obtain access to almost all documents of the government. Through the responsible judgements of editors and journalists, combined with consistentjudicial support, a tradition and culture of media freedom develops. This culture is, above all, the most important guarantor of media freedom and of the ability of the media to fullyoperate as a watchdog over public office holders.

The tradition must provide for the media tobe tough in its scrutiny of the work of those who enjoy the public trust. The media culture, as is evident in many democracies today, must involve a sense that it is the duty of the mediato afflict the comfortable (those holding public office), in order to comfort the afflicted (thepublic at large). There is no question that such a culture can, at times, lead to media irresponsibility. This is aninevitable price to pay. An independent, wise judiciary and an effective Press Council, may beable to assist in curbing excesses in such times. Nevertheless, societies should be willing to paysome price for the greater good of securing media freedom. The critical factor on all issues concerned with restricting freedom of the media is that the limitsbe publicly debated and that they be interpreted by a fully independent judiciary, composed of individuals of the highest integrity.

Perhaps even more ominous is self-censorship, where journalists and editors do not follow upstories that might upset business interests, the proprietors of the newspaper or those close to them. This can cause stories to be ignored or written in ways which are at best unethical. Self-censorshipcan range from the mundane (stories that are considered important but "dull" andare therefore not reported) to the heights of conflicts of interest with the news organisation (stories are unreported because they impact on advertisers or friends of these in influentialpositions in the paper). Fortunate, indeed, is the editor who has his Board sign off on a statement such as this:

> "Time-Warner's board, its chief executive, and the chief executive of Time Inc. recognisethat the financial success of Time Inc. 's magazines is inextricably linked to their credibility. The board and the chief executives hold the Editor-in-Chief of Time Inc. accountablefor the editorial quality and integrity of the company's magazines. To this end, theyare committed to upholding the Editor-in-Chief's unique level of independence. The publications under the Editor-in-Chief's control are expected to provide readerswith synthesis, analysis, review, and commentary. They are also expected to provideunbiased coverage of the myriad interests of advertisers and of Time Warneritself. Editorial independence is essential so that the Editor-in-Chief can producepublications that advance the public interest while delivering a superior returnon investment. . . "

PRINCIPLES

Governments should embrace a basic set of principles to govern approaches to the media. An example of such principles was set out in the Charter for a Free Press approved by journalists from 34 countries at the Voices of Freedom World Conference on Censorship Problems.

United Nations SecretaryGeneral, Boutros Boutros-Ghali, declared that "They (the Charter's principles)deserve the support of everyone pledged to advance and protect democraticinstitutions". He added that the provisions, while non-binding, express goals"to which all free nations aspire". The Charter reads:

- Censorship, direct or indirect, is unacceptable; thus laws and practices restricting the right of the news media freely to gather and distribute information must be abolished, and government authorities, national and local, must not interfere with the content of print or broadcast news, or restrict access to any news source.
- Independent news media, both print and broadcast, must be allowed to emerge and operate freely in all countries.
- There must be no discrimination by governments in their treatment, economic or otherwise, of the news media within a country. In those countries where government media also exist, the independent media must have the same free access as the official media have to all material and facilities necessary to their publishing or broadcasting operations.
- States must not restrict access to newsprint, printing facilities and distribution systems, operation of news agencies, and availability of broadcast frequencies and facilities.
- Legal, technical and tariff practices by communications authorities which inhibit the distribution of news and restrict the flow of information are condemned.
- Government media must enjoy editorial independence and be open to a diversity of viewpoints. This should be affirmed in both law and practice.
- There should be unrestricted access by the print and broadcast media within a country to outside news and

information services, and the public should enjoy similar freedom to receive foreign publications and foreign broadcasts without interference.

- National frontiers must be open to foreign journalists. Quotas must not apply, and applications for visas, press credentials and other documentation requisite for their work should be approved promptly. Foreign journalists should be allowed to travel freely within a country and have access to both official and unofficial news sources, and be allowed to import and export freely all necessary professional materials and equipment.
- Restrictions on the free entry to the field of journalism or over its practice, through licensing or other certification procedures, must be eliminated.
- Journalists, like all citizens, must be secure in their persons and be given full protection of law. Journalists working in war zones are recognised as civilians enjoying all rights and immunities accorded to other civilians.

Violence against journalists has taken place in scores of countries, and public authorities havetime and again indicated their unwillingness to do anything about it. The only meaningfulantidote to such behaviour is the existence of laws and systems that guarantee a free media. In Algeria and Colombia, for example, a considerable number of journalists have been murderedin recent years. The murderers have not been found and often the authorities have notdemonstrated great zeal in finding those who were responsible. In 1994, the Inter-AmericanPress Association General Assembly noted that a high proportion of the political prisoners inCuba were serving sentences for "divulging enemy propaganda; in the previous year ten journalistswere murdered in Colombia, four in Mexico, three in Guatemala and one in Brazil".

The declaration from the conference, held in Toronto, stated in part: "The withholding of government advertising, spurious lawsuits against the media, and intimidation by narcotraffickers all have the effect of putting a damper on thefree exercise of journalism." Discrimination by governments among different media--providing some journalists withgreater access to governmental information and greater effective independence of action--iscommonplace. It may take the overt form of governments providing preference in the accessto information for journalists working solely for state-owned media or it may take the slightlymore subtle form of exclusively providing advertising to government-owned media, or tomedia that adhere to governmental views.

The legal and regulatory powers enjoyed by government authorities are also often used tointimidate or censor the media. For example, the government can place constraints on mediainvolving quotas on the import of newsprint and the imposition of special taxes and postalrates, as well as restricting the broadcast frequencies available to independent electronicmedia. This is likely to become an issue of mounting importance as electronic mail and newinformation-communications technologies provide new opportunities for people to freelyexpress their views to wide audiences. Protection of sources is a core requirement for journalists to freely practise their profession. Journalists must know that they can print stories without risking fines or imprisonment forfailing to reveal their sources of information.

Individuals who provide journalists withinformation on an "off-the-record" basis need to have assurances that the journalists theyconfide in will not be intimidated by public authorities into revealing their identities. The seas surances are essential if the media is to be an effective counterforce to the abuse of powerby public officials. The licensing of journalists can take many forms and frequently represents atype of intimidation. In some countries, governments seek to regulate thelicensing of media enterprises and their employees directly, while elsewherethere may be media trade unions that seek to force restrictive practices ontheir members. Licensing practices do not serve the public interest. The eliminationof media licensing should embrace foreign correspondents; theyshould always have as much access to information and as much opportunityto practice their profession as do all other local journalists.

Although civil libel actions can be consistent with the notion of a free media, this is patently not the case with regard to criminal libel actions. Within thisframework it is important to consider anti-insult laws, which exist in numerouscountries unreasonably and oppressively to protect public office holders, even where libel laws (correctly) set lower levels of protection for these officialsrelative to private citizens. For example, in recent times numerous governments in Central Europe haveintroduced legislation which stipulates severe penalties for journalists whopublish articles that may be viewed as insulting holders of high governmental office. In some cases the laws make no distinction as to whether mediareports are truthful or not.

In other words, the fact that a journalist wrote thetruth about improper acts by leaders of the government would not be viewedby the courts as a defence in cases where anti-insult laws are applied. The selaws amount to forms of intimidation and censorship which can be particularlyadvantageous to corrupt officials. In this regard, anti-insult laws shouldbe subsumed within libel law. The courts need to recognise media intimidation for what it really is: a centralfacet of a culture of corruption and an effort by strong vested intereststo perpetuate their corrupt practices. All regulation of the media, in terms ofpermits, licences and ownership, should be conducted with total transparency, and by regulators who are independent and nonpartisan.

The burden of ensuring a responsible, independent media must be shouldered primarily by themedia itself. Journalists must work hard to build public regard. They must demonstrate theirindependence, objectivity and professionalism each and every day in order to earn public trustand confidence. At the same time, it is imperative that the owners of the media ensure thatjournalists are paid wages which encourage independence, rather than dependence. Numerous national and multi-national media organisations focus on the preservation of thefreedom of the media. The Press Foundation of Asia Committee, the Canadian Committee toProtect Journalists, the International Federation of Journalists and the World Press FreedomCommittee are but a few of the organisations which should be supported for their efforts tohelp governments put in place laws and arrangements that correspond with the dictates of theprinciples of a free media.

Major foundations—the Freedom Forum, the Reuters Foundation, the Knight-Ridder Foundationand numerous others—seek to secure appropriate journalistic training to raise the qualityof media output in those countries where journalistic training is limited. In the fight againstcorruption, journalists must hone their skills with regard to investigative reporting, understandpublic accountability systems, the operations of modern business, and, in particular, the recognitionof corrupt practices. Some indicators as to the effectiveness of the media as an integrity pillar

– Are there freedom of information laws and/or do procedures exist to ensure that members of the public can obtain information/documents from public authorities?

- Does the country have an "Official Secrets Act" or something similar--if so, is it used as a tool to effectively secure censorship of the media by government?
- Are libel laws used, in effect, to censor the media and curb the dissemination of information about persons who influence the community?
- Do journalists have to be licensed? If so, is this a device to effectively curb journalistic freedom?
- Is the publicly-owned media independent of government control as to editorial content? If not, is the publicly-owned media in practice relied upon, by the public at large, as a credible news source?
- Does the publicly-owned media routinely carry stories critical of the administration (e. g. quoting opposition politicians etc.)?

14

Communication Arrangements in the UN System

Effective communications are the lifeblood of a complex modern organization. The organization's ability to contribute in substantive terms to those goals also depends on its ability to communicate, for skill in communication is an essential attribute of leadership in organizations as in individuals. The United Nations' ability to define issues, set policy agendas, and promote constructive solutions are a function of its ability to make the case for the value of its ideas and actions. Public diplomacy is at the heart of its mission.

The kind of communications that allows an organization to be effective in its substantive work as well as its constituency-building can be characterized as strategic communications. Much of the dissatisfaction with the current public information activities of the United Nations Secretariat appear to spring from the perception that they are not contributing as much as they should to the Organization's ability to lead, or to building support among its crucial constituencies.

In other words, they are not strategic. Very few of the information activities of the UN Secretariat are designed to be strategic. They serve a very different--and very important--set of institutional functions: responding to the information needs of various constituencies (delegations, NGOs, media, educational institutions), carrying out the instructions of the General Assembly, creating and preserving the historical record of the Organization's work, facilitating public access to UN documents and records, publishing accounts of UN actions, creating channels for public participation in UN activities, and so forth. These form the substance of institutional communications.

The key difference between strategic and institutional communications is that the former proceeds from a fully developed sense of the direction in which the organization wants to move opinion. Various communications techniques are then enlisted to that end. Strategic communications involves a process that begins with identifying the what, the how, and the who (to whom are communications to be targeted; which NGOs, interest groups, parliamentarians, press organs, members of the policy community, elements of the general public?) of a concerted communications strategy. The guiding strategy is aimed at making the United Nations a more powerful and effective advocate for the programs, policies, and values its members seek to advance.

Without such a strategy, institutional communications are likely to be fragmented, reactive, and to have little cumulative impact on public opinion. Strategic communications aim not just to affect but to mobilize public and specialist opinion on behalf of the United Nations. There are a number of units within the Secretariat that have specialist responsibilities for public information.They are mentioned only in relation to the activities of the other four units or in the context of Secretariat communications.

The United Nations Secretariat, much less the UN system as a whole, has no overarching communications strategy that can bolster its leadership capacity and its public support. None of the four communications entities has the task and the current capacity to devise and implement such a strategy. In order to emerge with a strong and positive voice in international policy debates, the United Nations must win and hold the confidence of political and civil-society leaders and their publics. The ability of the Organization to promote particular issues and approaches depends, therefore, on the quality and coherence of its message.

Strategic communication is more than the sum of its parts, which include public information, press relations, and constituency-building. Above all, it is an intimate link in policy-making. The vision of the Organization's role and priorities that drives the communications effort must proceed from the top policy-making level and pervade the Organization comprehensively. In the meantime, however, the daily business of institutional communications must continue to provide information on the work of the Organization to the public and the UN's specialized constituencies.

The United Nations is respected by the public worldwide. In recent years, however, it has frequently had difficulties in translating that respect into support for its mission. This is despite the fact that most people in most countries still hold the organization in considerable regard most of the time. Where opinion polls have been conducted, a majority of those interviewed declare general support for the organization. Indeed in the United States, often thought to be home to the Organization's most persistent critics, more than 60 percent of Americans when polled routinely express support for the Organization. Although attitudes toward the UN are measured less frequently elsewhere, similar levels of support are visible.

Among thirty-eight countries polled by the UN's Department of Public Information (DPI) between 1989 and 1993, only in one country--a developing county, as it happens--were a narrow majority of respondents critical of the UN's performance. Elsewhere, friends were in the majority. The United Nations has been identified with some of the great issues of our time. From the drive to eliminate apartheid and prevent the proliferation of nuclear weapons, to promotion of human rights and the advancement of women, the UN has articulated standards, provided forums for negotiation, and developed instruments for action.

The United Nations' growing distance from ordinary people, in the industrialized countries in particular, seems explicable at several levels. Region by region, there have been blows to the UN's operational reputation, many of them linked to the perceived inability of the Security Council, the most visible of the UN political bodies, to act decisively on major issues. So for example in Europe, the failure to protect the safe haven of Srebrenica and the handling of the Bosnian crisis more generally still weigh heavily on the UN.

A more lasting difficulty is that in some countries the UN is not considered relevant to the issues people care most about. This is despite poll findings around the world that health, disaster relief, the environment, food security, human rights, crime and drugs score highly as issues that people understand must be addressed internationally. UN agencies and programs address each of them. Yet, in many countries, the UN's ownership of these issues is not acknowledged by public opinion. Equally, the UN is considered marginal to the everyday economic problems that also dominate poll results in developing and developed countries: people do not find effective operational solutions for job and income problems from the UN.

There is a lesson to be learned from those countries where the UN's relevance is not doubted, such as low income countries where UN development activities are visible and important; or countries afflicted by or emerging from conflict where the UN's political, humanitarian, and reconstruction roles have been central. In these cases we do not need polling data to know that the UN matters. People hold passionate views about the organization and its relevance. Beyond the circle of countries where effective UN programs can be seen in operation, however, the UN is seen as a distant "talking shop" rather than an organization that can bring solutions that matter to "me"--me as an individual, my family, my community, my country.

At a time of rapid, unsettling global change, the UN's agenda, while theoretically relevant, does not seem to unleash the action that people expect in order to reduce the sense of insecurity that has accompanied these changes. It "resolutions" appear to have little impact on--sometimes, indeed, no relationship at all to--how individuals view change and seek to manage it. There is a particular irony in this disconnect, because the United Nations, in a de facto alliance with civil society, has played a large role in expanding public consciousness of global issues such as environmental change, gender equity, population and human rights--issues which are perceived as relevant to individual concerns.

Less than ten years ago only a billion people lived in market-oriented societies, now 5 billion do; in 1974, thirty-nine countries elected their national leaderships, today 117 do. Yet viewed from the perspectives of many individual citizens, the UN is not seen as playing a central role in the new equation. The effect of globalization has been to leave people in awe of the power of global economic trends and skeptical about the ability of their national authorities--much less multilateral institutions-- to mitigate or manage those trends in a way that will protect individuals and what they hold dear.

To the extent the UN does register, polls commissioned by the UN Department of Public Information in 1989-93 in 38 countries showed that UNICEF and UNESCO had more impact on public opinion than the Security Council, the General Assembly, or even at that time the Secretary-General. Today it seems likely that agencies or programs such as UNHCR in the Great Lakes and Bosnia or UNAIDS, in areas where it is actively marketing preventive health approaches, will have more reputational impact than the UN itself. More generally, regional polling data suggests the UN's institutional reputation is often not free-standing but follows respect for national government and regional organizations.

Where these are respected they provide "coat tails" that lift support for the more distant, less understood United Nations; where, as is often the case today, there is declining respect for government and regional institutions and their ability to mitigate the effect of global economic change, then, inevitably it weakens support for that shadowy, weak global layer of governance that lies behind national and regional institutions. So at a time when the UN's unique international role and agenda, and the values it articulates, coincide with the concerns of people in both industrialized and developing countries, one might expect it to have a place at the center of peoples' world view. In fact, the opposite has happened. Among many, there is respect and fondness for what the UN was set up to do, but little sense of current relevance.

UN's Advantages

An organization that is viewed as distant and not relevant to the problems and concerns of "me"--myself, my family, community and country--is one that is quickly tagged in the public's mind as a vast, unaccountable, ineffective bureaucracy. Further, no amount of good communications is going to lift this reputation unless there is seen to be major change in the Organization's performance. The reform program is the threshold requirement for restoring public respect. Effective communications and organizational change are inseparable: communications will only be credible coming from a UN that is seen to have changed.

Moreover, vigorous communications can promote that change--inside and outside the organization. That said, the UN has considerable natural assets in a world which is more integrated in terms of ideas, commerce, investment, and communications than at any time in history. First, the UN has one of the world's great mission statements, its Charter, a document that remains as contemporary today as it was when it was written more than 50 years ago. It remains a great rallying cry for common approaches to world issues. Second, the UN has the unique global capacity to frame issues, stimulate global debate about those issues, and forge a consensus around them.

Interest groups, opposition movements, religious leaders, social activists, policy makers, and peoples of all persuasions, ideologies, and causes beat their way to the UN's doors because it remains the great global launching-pad for big ideas, where governmental decision-makers pay attention. Whether at the world conferences in Beijing or Copenhagen, Cairo or Rio de Janeiro, the UN demonstrated its ability to draw global attention to an issue and see that it is debated by both government officials and representatives of civil society. While these conferences were criticized at the time by some for their apparent devotion to talk rather than action, they represent the culmination of decades-long processes which have effectively produced significant changes in perception and consciousness, leaving a lasting impact on the course of global policy-making.

While the UN succeeded in introducing new norms into the global debate; it is often national actors who have brought these successes home to people in their own lives. So local champions take the credit in citizens' eyes, and the distant UN basks only in reflected glory. The UN provides an extraordinary forum for debate and consensus building, together with a subsequent capacity to serve as an advocate for action and a framework for implementation of action on that new consensus. This is a unique and valuable role which belies the perception of a worthy but ineffectual talking shop. The UN has played this role on the environment, women's issues, social development and other issues with some effect. It is the world's communications agency.

Whereas in many of its areas of operational activity it faces local, regional and international competitors who may have more resources, expertise and capacity, in its communications role the UN enjoys a unique stature. The world is no longer as divided by competing agendas as it was. The old divide in which the "southern" UN agenda revolved around development issues such as poverty and debt while the "north" looked to the UN primarily on political matters is largely gone. While views on solutions may often differ, there is growing agreement on what the agenda should be. The agenda encompasses issues of development and conflict resolution, but stretches to include humanitarian issues, gender issues, population and environment among other matters.

The priorities are being driven by the shared problems and concerns that individual, families and communities are facing everywhere. These issues do not stop at national borders. The UN's natural advantages occur at a moment of new opportunity: Two changes that are sweeping the world offer new reach to the UN's communications role. First, the extraordinary rise of civil society offers new global and national networks of citizens for the UN to communicate with, and through. It is a time of explosive growth in both numbers and recognition of such organizations. As national governments have discovered, civil society provides scope for creative partnerships which the UN is well-placed to seize.

Although there are different opinions on the ways and means of developing this relationship, the possibilities have expanded greatly in the last decade. Second, there are equally significant changes taking place in the character of global information flows--some of which promote the opportunity for more effective UN communications and some of which place barriers in its way. On the positive side, the volume of information being shared among societies and people has grown dramatically, whether it is the need of financial traders in Frankfurt, Shanghai, or Lima to access the same real-time global information services; individuals meeting across the Internet around shared interests; or the rise of global television services.

The rise of customized information exchange via the Internet, talk radio, newsletters and other media, together with the power of modern mass culture to reach across societies when traditional foreign news reporting by many national TV and press outlets is declining, takes us back to the principal theme of this report: information must relate meaningfully to the individual and his or her family or community. Many newspaper and television editors have acknowledged a re-focusing of foreign news away from stories about politics and governments to features about life style, culture, and shared issues such as the environment or human rights. The global story still works when it is placed in a meaningful local context for the reader or viewer.

A report sponsored by the Council on Foreign Relations in the United State observed:

> "The United Nations should be intelligible to its varied constituencies. Voting publics must understand the United Nations if they are to support it. The vigorous and hazardous work of U.N. personnel in the field--in health care delivery, refugee work, peacekeeping, and development assistance--often is less visible than the political functions. The same is true of essential U.N. agencies that regulate maritime and aviation safety, allocate radio communications spectra, and undertake world wide weather reporting to track hurricanes and disasters. The United Nations should overhaul its Department of Public Information and make information about U.N. operations more accessible to the American press and public. A "political unbundling" would allow church and evangelical groups, American corporations, environmental organizations, transportation safety groups, and other citizen associations to identify the U.N. operations that enhance their own international efforts."

The UN's communications challenge is evident: putting itself and its program back in touch with people; demonstrating that its agenda is their agenda. Certain over-riding principles that must, drive this change:

— *There is an over-used maxim in communications:* think globally, act locally. It endures, however, because it remains an important insight. The communications function of the UN must be organized around a strong central design that allows all activities to reinforce rather than contradict or weaken each other. At the same time that there is coordination of the global message and position together with much more effective central implementation capacity than in the past, there must also be a high degree of effective delegation to an empowered and effective country-level UN communications program. This will allow the translation of global messages and campaigns into ones that are effective locally; that meet the challenge of relevance.

— *Everybody must be a communicator:* If one of the core strengths of the UN is as a communications agency, then the communications function cannot be devolved solely to a single specialist department. Rather, the "communications culture" must infiltrate the work program, job descriptions and responsibilities of all senior UN staff. Public diplomacy, as the communications function is now widely described, must be at the heart of the Organization's mission. Making the UN's case to the public must become a key and accepted part of official responsibilities. This emphasis on public diplomacy--making the wider case--must not stop at the door of the Secretariat. Ambassadors, agencies, and programs--that is, the broader UN family-- must become full campaigners in this effort. In that sense the communications department's role is as a facilitator, organizer and promoter for the UN's communications activities.

— *The pre-eminent role of issues:* There must be a strategic determination to conduct overlapping, sequential campaigns on certain issues that have relevance to audiences across the world. These must not be vague abstracts but "wedge" issues that are designed to force actions on the environment, poverty, drugs, employment, or other matters of concern to member states. These communications campaigns would be tied to the General Assembly and must draw in the full UN system. On many issues, it is the agencies or programs, not the Secretariat, which have more public credibility.

— *The central role of the Secretary-General:* Concern has been expressed that the Secretary-General is being asked to undertake too many public activities, and that this is both over-stretching him and risking an over-personalization of the UN's reputation. However, the UN's Preparatory Commission fifty years ago pointed out that "The Secretary-General, more than anyone else, will stand for the United Nations as a whole. In the eyes of the world, he must embody the principles and ideals of the UN Charter to which the Organization seeks to give effect".(2) Organizations in the modern media environment often are strongly associated with the public persona of the chief executive, and this can give clarity to a complex public image. There is, in addition, a growing group of other attractive and articulate UN leaders and spokespersons who should be fully utilized and developed.

— Placing the communications planning function with the General Assembly, and the Committee on Information, on an appropriate strategic level. This must enable the Committee to direct the overall work program by reviewing goals and campaign themes while not fragmenting the work program with mandates that cannot be serviced with existing resources. The Committee might consider a single-mandate approach which lays out goals and priorities and then leaves management to determine how best to deploy resources to achieve those objectives. The Committee's strategic and directional role would also include evaluation of how well strategies are being implemented.

— There must be a flexibility to focus resources and effort on priority targets at particular times. Currently that would include a strong issue-based effort to persuade US public opinion, and the more skeptical US political and policy elite, that the UN is deeply relevant to American concerns. Nevertheless these efforts should be run within the overall communications strategy. In our opinion, progress will be driven primarily by strong implementation at the local and national level of global UN campaigns and messages that demonstrate relevance, rather than through distinct and separate efforts.

— *The UN's institutional image must be addressed*: At the moment, the limited public understanding of the UN's role has reduced the strong positive attribute of a global communications agency to a negative--a "talking-shop" that does not gets things done. The UN must delineate, in its communications, the two separate functions that give it its unique stature. First, it is a unique global forum for debate, reflection and ultimate consensus; second, through the Secretary-General, the Secretariat, the inter-governmental bodies, and other parts of the system, it is advocate and implementer of that consensus. An institutional image which reflects these two steps--debate followed by action-- will be much stronger than the blurred, inconsistent image that has muddled present public understanding in many parts of the world.

Department of Public Information (DPI)

The communications environment in which the United Nations operates today is very different from that of 1946, when the first session of the General Assembly established the Department of Public Information (DPI). Today, DPI remains the centerpiece and by far the largest implementer of institutional communications in the UN Secretariat. Its budget of about $71 million per year dwarfs that of the other units with communications responsibilities, as does its 861-member staff.

DPI serves many masters. It is directed by and reports to both the Secretary-General and the General Assembly. It serves the Secretariat, other agencies and programs of the UN system, the delegations, certain regional organizations, the press, educational institutions, non-governmental organizations, and the general public. Each of these, not surprisingly, tends to feel that its requirements should be given highest priority, and to disparage DPI for not being more responsive to its particular needs. DPI is the center of the UN's institutional communications.

Ironically, for a department charged with public information, DPI has not been effective at informing the public, or even other parts of the UN Secretariat, about what it does. The work of the Department and the constraints under which it operates are little understood. Nor are the considerable changes that the Department has undergone in the last several years. Most notably, as members of the Task force talked to journalists and other users of DPI services, such as diplomatic missions and NGOs. None of them seemed to feel well-served; every user felt short-changed when they compared the level of service they were getting to what they would expect from an 861-person department with a $71 million annual budget. And they imagined it was because others were getting a quality of service denied to them.

On DPI's side, there was not a single service or unit whose staff did not consider it under-resourced. Many offices felt they no longer had the resources to get the job done; all felt they lacked the financial means to deliver an effective program. The truth seems to be that DPI's resources are so dispersed and its work program so driven by multiple mandates given it by governments that there is not the critical mass of effort around key priorities that would satisfy any one of DPI's constituencies that it was getting an adequate depth of service. The Department is organized into six major units. These include the office of the Assistant Secretary-General; three divisions, each comprising a number of services and sections; and one free-standing service, the Information Centres Service.

The Department of Public Information had a budget of approximately $143 million for the 1996-97 biennium, including nearly $5 million in extra-budgetary resources and about $2 million for the Spokesman's Office. Thus, the DPI budget represents about 5.5 per cent of the regular budget for the "core" United Nations. Its staff of 861, 10 of whom are attached to the Spokesman's Office, makes up 8.5 per cent of the core UN staff of 10,021.

Media Division

With 25 per cent of the DPI budget and 17 per cent of its staff, the Media Division provides services to the media that cover the UN, such as press accreditation, written summaries of the proceedings of official meetings, film footage of meetings and events for use by television broadcasters, current and archival photographs, and daily digests of events at the UN. Broadcasters may also subscribe to video packages of daily highlights.

The AP, Reuters, Worldwide TV News and CNN are among the subscribers. The income from sales of television news coverage amounts to about $700,000 in this biennium, but does not cover costs. The Media Division also produces finished products for radio and television broadcast. Television products include:

— "Questions and answers about the UN": 30-second spots.

— "UN Minutes": 60-second spots on moments of UN history

— "UN in Action": 3-minute mini-features on the work of the UN and the specialized agencies around the world. About 60 segments are produced annually. Available by subscription, they reach an estimated audience of 200 million a week, and are regularly included in the CNN World Report.

— "Year in Review": a 15-minute program produced annually showing highlights of the Organization's activities and major events.

— "World Chronicle": a 30-minute weekly talk-show in which UN officials and other experts are interviewed by a panel of journalists.

In addition, over 100 films and videos are currently in active distribution, of which at least 21 have won film-festival prizes. Some cover UN activities, while other cover subjects of concern to the UN--the decolonization of Namibia and Zimbabwe, landmines, and the Central American Peace process are examples. Still others are part of the observance of particular UN days, years, or decades. Some films generate substantial revenue.

Radio programs are made in the six official UN languages and nine others. Programming is roughly 40 per cent news and 60 per cent feature material. Most of the production is in the form of taped programs, which are mailed to broadcasters. This means of delivery is highly problematic, resulting in late arrival of many programs, some of which are outdated by the time they are received. A proposal is being developed for a direct broadcast service, which would obviate delivery problems. Already there is more direct broadcasting through telephone and digital lines, and attempts are being made to make fuller use of the Internet.

An audio news service is available by telephone 24 hours a day, but a recent evaluation suggested that it was used more by delegations and NGOs than the press. Programming in recent years has been refocused on peace-keeping operations, especially when a new operation is launched in a hostile environment.

Library and Publications Division

This division runs the Dag Hammarskjold Library and produces a number of Secretariat publications such as the quarterlies UN Chronicle and Africa Recovery, the UN Yearbook, and the Blue Book series. It includes the sales and marketing section, and has been assigned the lead implementing role in the Department's remarkably rapid and successful adoption of advanced information technology, including its presence on the world wide web. The division accounts for 23 per cent of the DPI budget and 24 per cent of its staff.

The Library is mandated to acquire and maintain a complete collection of all UN documents and publications issued in any language anywhere in the world, to provide complete bibliographic access to them, and to maintain a global network of depository libraries. It is also required to keep a collection of non-UN publications that are relevant to the Organization's work, and to help the Secretariat staff, delegates and permanent missions obtain the information they need in the course of their work. The Library has made great strides in digitalizing the vast quantity of documentation generated by the UN, and in making it widely available in electronic form.

In addition to the periodicals and books mentioned above, the Publications Service regularly produces eight other publications. One of them, the twice-monthly Development Business more than meets its operational costs through subscription to its printed and on-line versions. Others include the Annual Report of the Secretary-General, Basic Facts About the United Nations, and UN in Brief. The Service includes a design section which serves all Secretariat publications, an editorial section, and a production and coordination section which coordinates production for all print products in the Secretariat. The Division has also responded to in-house demand for Internet training, offering instruction to over 1000 people from the missions and the Secretariat, so far.

Promotion and Public Services Division

This division responds to a number of General Assembly/

Committee on Information mandates to promote the work of the United Nations around particular themes, events and observances, such as the major world conferences on environment, population, women, social development, and so forth. It sees itself as the "think tank" of DPI, planning campaigns to incorporate special events and particular constituencies into the overall public information program of the UN.

The division also organizes the direct contact between the United Nations and members of the general public, through tours, exhibits, and responses to 90,000 public inquiries per year. Public Liaison includes an NGO liaison service for 1500 NGOs accredited to DPI, which gives these organizations access to information about UN activities and a channel for participation in some of them. There are weekly briefings for NGOs, and an annual conference at Headquarters. Recently, the division has been given responsibility for responding to misinformation about the United Nations, publishing quick and timely fact sheets that correct common misperceptions.

The Promotion and Public Services Division also acts as the secretariat to the Joint United Nations Information Committee (JUNIC), which brings together officials responsible for public information throughout the UN system so that they can coordinate their efforts. The budget of the division accounts for 8 per cent of DPI funds and 6 per cent of its staff.

Information Centres Service and the UNICs

The Information Centres Service coordinates, administers, and services the network of UN Secretariat information centers and services outside of New York. The 61 UN Information Centers (UNICs) in as many countries, and the UN Information Services in Geneva and Vienna, together account for 35 per cent of the information budget, and 44 per cent of posts. Central support for the UNICs, provided by the Information Centres Service, accounts for an additional 3 per cent of DPI's budget and another 3 per cent of its staff. The UNICs are the local conduit for information from and about the United Nations. They organize press conferences, seminars, exhibits, and other events to promote UN reports, conferences or observances. They adapt UN information materials into local languages.

In some cases the UNICs work with local media outlets to advance the understanding of UN programs and positions, especially on matters of regional or local interest. Some are able to produce press releases and other materials in local languages for use by the press and the general public. Many maintain reference libraries, including audio-visual resources, and facilitate model-UN programs. Most maintain liaison with local non-governmental associations, including UN Associations. In information, one size does not fit all, so the UNICs have the task of tailoring and targeting information as appropriate in their particular setting.

In addition to disseminating UN information, the UNICs provide feedback to UN Headquarters on national and regional trends, and on local media coverage of the UN. Many UNICs will handle logistical arrangements and media liaison for senior UN officials during local visits. They may be called upon to perform representational duties, or even such services as inspecting airplanes for compliance with UN embargoes.

The number of field information offices has grown while the resources for them have not. Since the late 1980s, nearly half of the UNICs have been integrated into the office of the UN Resident Co-ordinator, in the name of efficiency and for the sake of presenting a unified image of the UN system. Substantial problems have arisen as a result. In some centers, DPI reports that information activities have dropped off alarmingly. Nor have the expected cost savings necessarily materialized, as the UNIC component pays a smaller share of a larger total for facilities that may not suit its purposes. The problems of integration have proved difficult to correct. DPI has no part in evaluating the performance of UN Resident Coordinators who have UNIC responsibilities, and some Co-ordinators are unresponsive to DPI requests and programming. A joint DPI/UNDP working group and other efforts have not resolved the problems so far.

There are a number of specific constraints on DPI activities, which fall into three categories: those imposed by member states, those resulting from resource levels, and those that flow from the bureaucratic practices and procedures of the Secretariat. Servicing the multiple users of information about the United Nations in response to the specific instructions of the Committee on Information makes heavy demands on the staff and budget of DPI. Although the resolution establishing the Department assigns responsibility for the formulation and execution of information policy to the Secretary-General, "subject to the general authority of the principal organs of the United Nations", the Committee on Information has in many ways replaced the Secretary-General's role by approving many detailed mandates for the Department.

Currently, DPI labors under more than 350 General Assembly/Committee on Information mandates, many of which tell the Department not only what to do but how, in very specific terms, to do it. More than half of the 49th General Assembly's resolutions containing requests for public information services asked for specific services or products, rather than specifying an objective and letting DPI managers judge the best way of accomplishing it. Since few of these mandates have "sunset" provisions, their accumulated weight deprives the Department of flexibility and responsiveness.

For example, about one-third of the mandates adopted at the 44th session of the General Assembly, while not restated since, are still current. DPI is currently responsible for the mandated observance of 21 international days and weeks, 13 decades, and five international years. In 1995, it was instructed to publicize a total of 65 conferences and observances. Some progress has been made through negotiations between the Committee and the Department to streamline some of the mandates. But much more needs to be done to ease the burden of micro- management. DPI has learned to do more with less in recent years, largely through the creative application of new technology.

The personnel system throws up two kinds of obstacles to efficient management of resources. One is the "last in-first out" system of contracts, in which newly created positions often tend initially to be filled only on the basis of very short term contracts. In DPI, the newly created positions tend to be the technology related ones, in which the relevant skills are scarce and in high demand. The inability to offer even short-term job security and reasonable career development prospects makes it difficult to hire good people with these sought-after skills.

Secondly, junior professional (P1/P2) posts in the UN are filled only by competitive exam, and it is impossible for a manager to specify precisely what skills are needed in his/her division. Rigidities in the personnel process often prevent managers from hiring the kind of person they think best qualified for the job at more senior levels as well. The extreme slowness and inefficiency of UN procurement has kept services such as publications, marketing and library user services waiting for months for equipment that would allow them to do more and better work with the same or fewer people, in less time. Even after funds have been appropriated and assigned, the wait continues, punctuated by repeated demands to justify the acquisition of the already-approved equipment.

Managers often feel that they could buy what they need off-the-shelf, instantly, for less money. Many of the computers are more than five years old, during which time technology has progressed by leaps and bounds. Investments are not made that could literally pay for themselves, such as just-in-time printing technology which can obviate the need to maintain large inventories of publications or documents. Slow procurement runs the risk that what is acquired will be out of date before it is installed. The rigidity of budgeting practices prevents managers from shifting resources (human or financial) from areas where needs have declined to tasks that could put more resources to productive use. In addition, revenue generation is completely divorced from investment.

Services that could pay for themselves cannot borrow against future revenues, or even use money they earn to expand revenue-generating activities, because all earned income goes into the general account. This results in real absurdities, like the sales section being unable to fill a large rush order because it had no money to pay overtime, even though the resulting sales would more than cover the cost of the extra labor. The balance of needs for personnel, program, and equipment may shift dramatically within a biennium. Salaries and staff costs consume about 76 per cent of the DPI budget in the 1996-7 biennium.

In some services, so little money is available for supplies and equipment, travel, or general operating expenses that staff are less than fully occupied. Photographers cannot go out into the field to take pictures of UN programs; camera operators lack film reels, cartographers lack computer hardware. Yet it is impossible to re-program funds allocated for underutilized posts to pay for other, more pressing needs. The Spokesman's Office is the UN Secretariat's main interface with the working press, and its primary focus is the daily news cycle. While DPI, and in particular its Media Division, also provides certain services to the news media, such as meetings summaries and press kits for major conferences, most journalists do not regard it as a news resource.

They may use documents for background purposes, but most material arrives too late to be useful in covering breaking news. The exception is the audio and video tape coverage of events and meetings in New York and Geneva, which many broadcasters find useful, although they say that it is overly bureaucratic. It is the Spokesman's Office, however, that speaks to the press on behalf of the Secretary-General about newsworthy events in the Secretariat and those elsewhere on which he wishes to comment.

The Spokesman briefs the press and the delegations daily, on the record, and responds to press inquiries throughout the day. The Office is said to have become much more news-oriented in the past three years, and to have better access to information within the Secretariat . The staff is now more systematically deployed to keep up with events in the departments most likely to make news. It is severely handicapped, however, by a shortage of staff, which makes it impossible for the office to respond to many press inquiries in a timely fashion or to search out information from the substantive departments in order to give informed answers.

The number of posts assigned to the Spokesman's Office is not adequate to staff a serious news operation, and a number of the posts have been vacant for several months, including that of Deputy Spokesman. Since the Spokesman routinely travels with the Secretary-General, the Office is often down to only two professionals if the Spokesman is traveling and another officer is in a meeting, sick, or on leave. This is a source of considerable frustration to the media, especially those who are based at the UN, and often means that the Organization's views and positions simply go unreported.

The Spokesman's Office has a budget that amounts to about 1.4 per cent of the DPI budget, and has 1.2 per cent of its staff. Although it is administratively part of DPI, the Office has little contact with the rest of the Department in the course of its daily work. There is minimal coordination between them, in large part because their responsibilities are not seen to overlap.

The Assistant Secretary-General for External Affairs serves as a focal point for outreach to civil society. The emphasis that her office places on the host country, the United States, is presumably imposed by funding and staffing constraints as well as perceived needs. The office has only four staff, and is part of the Office of the Secretary-General. This office is the newest of the communications entities within the Secretariat, and sees its task as mobilizing support for the United Nations among major organs of civil society such as labor unions, business and professional associations, academic institutions, foundations, private voluntary organizations and such, reaching beyond the traditional NGO constituencies of the United Nations. And it is pro-active, seeking opportunities to boost the image of the United Nations before important audiences.

The Assistant Secretary-General therefore has an input in scheduling his appearances, working with the Spokesman's Office to vet media interviews. She also works with the speech writer's office on depth, coherence, and continuity in the message communicated through the Secretary-General's public appearances.

Caution was expressed elsewhere about focusing too heavily on the Secretary-General, putting the man ahead of the message or even the policy. The Assitant Secretary-General for External Affairs would like to see other senior

UN officials actively represent the UN to the public, while admitting that at this point in the new UN administration, most groups are only interested in having the Secretary-General himself. Thus, a major constraint on the activity of this office is the limited time of the principal and the heavy demands on him from other official duties. Currently, some 90 per cent of the invitations that come to him must be turned down.

Speechwriting Unit: The Speechwriting Unit is staffed by three English-language speech writers and two who write in French. All of the Secretary-General's scripted public statements pass through this office. It works with the Chief of Staff, the Spokesman's Office, and the substantive departments to develop the Secretary-General's statements.

The lack of a coherent strategy for communications, and even for the use of the Secretary-General's time, is felt to be a constraint on the effectiveness of the Speechwriting unit. The ad hoc decision-making of the moment involves too many contending voices giving different advice, overtaxing the Secretary-General's time and generating little cumulative impact. However, it is felt that some consistent themes are beginning to emerge across speeches, such as the need for reform, an emphasis on civil society, the relationship between development and the private sector, and the challenge of new, transnational issues such as the environment and ethnic conflict.

Index